Collins

AQA GCSE 9-1
Chemistry

Sam Holyman

Exam Skills
and **Practice**

How to use this book

This Exam Skills and Practice book puts the spotlight on the different types of command word – the instructional word or phrase in a question – you can expect to find in your GCSE papers. Each section has worked examples and lots of timed practice to help build your exam technique.

Top Tips offer nuggets of information to keep in mind when answering each type of question.

Scan the **QR code** to test your understanding of the command word and see worked solutions to the example question(s) on that page.

Each question shows the paper **P1 P2**, the part of the specification and grade range you are working at. Look out for maths skills 🖩 and practical skills 🔬 being tested.

Complete the example to take the next step in your practice. Parts of the workings and/or answers are given for you to finish. Helpful hints also steer you in the right direction.

Each **command word** is defined in easy-to-understand language.

Example questions show the command words in context. Use the QR code to access worked video solutions and commentary for them.

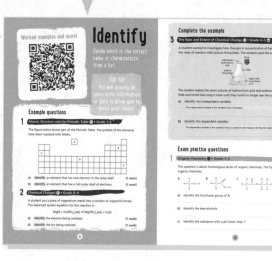

Exam practice questions enable you to delve deeper into each command word across a range of topics and grade levels. There is a target time for doing these at exam speed.

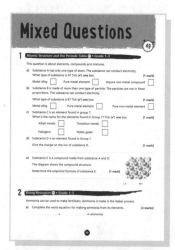

Mixed questions help to refine your exam skills with practice that recaps a variety of the command words.

An **index of topics** enables you to quickly find questions within the book from particular parts of the AQA GCSE specification.

Answers are given at the back of the book so that you can check and mark your own work.

Contents

Revise by command word!

Choose

Select your answer from a list of alternatives. These questions are usually targeted at lower grades.

TOP TIP
Select from the options given; do not use your own words.

Example questions

1 Chemical Changes P1 • Grade 1–3

Complete the sentences.

Choose answers from the box.   **[3 marks]**

| chemical | oxidation | oxygen | reduction | respiration |

.... reactions happen when a new substance is made.

.... is an example of a chemical reaction where a substance

gains ....

2 Energy Changes P1 • Grade 4–5

Charcoal is a fuel that can be combusted. This is an exothermic reaction. The figure on the right shows the reaction profile for the combustion of charcoal. What do labels A, B, C and D represent?

Choose answers from the box.   **[4 marks]**

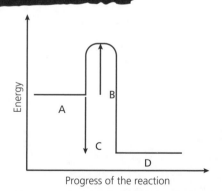

| reactant | product | activation energy | overall energy change |
| time | energy | catalyst |

Complete the example

3   Organic Chemistry ② • Grade 4–5

Chemists are able to take organic molecules and modify them in many ways to make new and useful materials.

Complete the sentences.

Choose answers from the box.

[3 marks]

alkane	alcohol	alkene	carboxylic acid
	crude oil	ester	hydrocarbon

Carboxylic acid is a weak acid. When an .... reacts with

.... , a sweet smelling .... is made.

Exam practice questions

1   Bonding, Structure, and the Properties of Matter ① • Grade 1–3

Substances can change state when they are heated or cooled.

The figure below shows the changes of state.

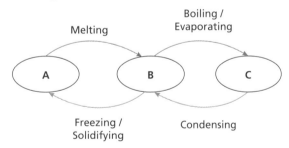

What do labels A, B and C represent?

Choose answers from the box.

[3 marks]

alloy	gas	liquid	solid

A = ...

B = ...

C = ...

2 Chemical Analysis ② • Grade 1–3

In the electrolysis of sodium chloride solution, NaCl(aq), bubbles were seen at each electrode. Both gases were collected and tested.

Complete the sentences.

Choose answers from the box. **[2 marks]**

| carbon dioxide | chlorine | hydrogen | oxygen |

The gas collected from the anode changed damp litmus paper white, so the gas was

....

The gas collected from the cathode burned rapidly with a pop sound, so the gas was

....

3 Energy Changes ① • Grade 1–3 ⊕

A student investigated a chemical reaction between hydrochloric acid and a metal powder.

The figure below shows a diagram of the equipment that they used.

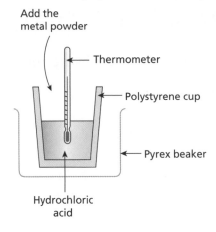

Add the
metal powder

Thermometer

Polystyrene cup

Pyrex beaker

Hydrochloric
acid

a) Complete the sentence about the results from the practical.

Choose the answer from the box. **[1 mark]**

| decreased | increased | stayed the same |

During the experiment, the temperature ....

b) Complete the sentence to give a conclusion from the practical.

Choose the answer from the box. **[1 mark]**

| an endothermic | an exothermic | a physical |

The experiment is an example of .... change.

4 Chemical Changes **P1** • Grade 4–5 🔒

A student can make a pure, dry sample of copper(II) sulfate by reacting copper(II) oxide.

Complete the sentences to explain the steps in the practical.

Choose the answers from the box.   **[4 marks]**

boiling	condensing	decrease	evaporating	excess
increase	filtrate	limiting	residue	

Sulfuric acid is heated up to .... the rate of reaction. As the

sulfuric acid is the .... reagent, the reaction mixture is filtered

to remove the .... copper(II) oxide. The copper(II) sulfate crystals

are obtained from the filtrate by .... the water.

5 Chemistry of the Atmosphere **P2** • Grade 4–5

For 200 million years, the proportions of different gases in the atmosphere have been much the same as they are today.

The figure below is a pie chart which shows the composition of dry air.

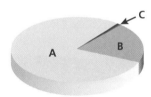

What do labels A, B and C represent?

Choose answers from the box.   **[3 marks]**

hydrogen	nitrogen	oxygen	water
carbon dioxide	oxygen	chlorine	

A = ...

B = ...

C = ...

Total score: .... / 14

Give

Only a short answer is required, not an explanation or a description.

Worked examples and more!

TOP TIP
Read the question carefully.

Example questions

1 **Energy Changes** P1 • Grade 1–3

There are three types of chemical cell that can be used to power a doorbell. The table below gives some information about each type of chemical cell.

	Alkaline battery	Zinc-carbon battery	Nickel-metal hydride battery
Rechargeable	No	No	Yes
Number of years before it needs replacing or recharging	1	0.5	0.7
Cost (UK pounds)	0.80	0.44	2.40

Give **one** advantage for each type of chemical cell. **[3 marks]**

2 **Bonding, Structure, and the Properties of Matter** P1 • Grade 4–5

Fullerenes are molecules of carbon atoms with hollow shapes.

a) Give the name of the first fullerene that was discovered. **[1 mark]**

b) Give **one** use of this fullerene. **[1 mark]**

Complete the example

3 Atomic Structure and the Periodic Table ⓟ • Grade 6–7

This question is about Group 1 metals and their reactions.

a) Give **two** observations you could make when a small piece of sodium is added to water. **[2 marks]**

> What do you see and hear during this experiment? Only write observations, not conclusions. For example, bubbles allow you to conclude that a gas is made and you might know it is hydrogen, but you would not get the mark for writing 'hydrogen gas was made', as it is not an observation.

1. ....

....

2. ....

....

b) Give the formula of the gaseous product of this reaction. **[1 mark]**

> Read the question carefully: the answer is a formula not a name. Even though there is a whole line for this answer, just write the formula. You do not have to fill the line. Remember all numbers in this formula should be subscript.

Exam practice questions

1 Organic Chemistry ⓟ / Chemistry of the Atmosphere ⓟ • Grade 1–3

Coal is a fossil fuel that is burned to provide heat in our homes.

a) Give the name of the gas used in the combustion of coal. **[1 mark]**

....

b) Give the name of the greenhouse gas that is made when coal is used. **[1 mark]**

....

c) Sulfur impurities can be found in coal that release acidic gases when it is used.

Give the name of pollution that this causes. **[1 mark]**

....

2   Atomic Structure and the Periodic Table ⓟ • Grade 4–5

An isotope of sodium can be represented by the symbol $^{24}_{11}Na$.

Give the number of each subatomic particle in this atom of sodium.   **[2 marks]**

Protons: ....

Neutrons: ....

Electrons: ....

3   Atomic Structure and the Periodic Table ⓟ • Grade 4–5

The elements in Group 7 and Group 1 can react together to make ionic compounds.

Group 1 metals are all examples of alkali metals.

a)   Give the name used to describe all elements in Group 7.   **[1 mark]**

....

b)   Group 7 elements make molecules consisting of two atoms.

Give the formula of a molecule of chlorine.   **[1 mark]**

....

c)   Give the formula of the ions formed when potassium and bromine react to
form an ionic compound.   **[2 marks]**

....

4   Chemical Analysis ⓟ • Grade 6–7 ☻

A student investigated the colours of some food colourings.

The diagram shows the equipment used.

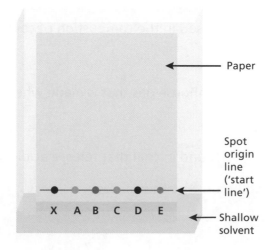

Paper

Spot origin line ('start line')

X   A   B   C   D   E

Shallow solvent

This is the method used:

1. Draw a 'start line', in pencil, on a piece of absorbent paper.

2. Put samples of five known food colourings (A, B, C, D and E) and the unknown substance (X) on the 'start line'.

3. Dip the edge of the paper into the water, ensuring the water level is below the start line.

4. Wait for the solvent to travel to the top of the paper.

5. Identify substance X by comparing the horizontal spots with the results of A, B, C, D and E.

Give **one** reason for:

*   Step 1
*   Step 3   [2 marks]

Step 1 ....

....

Step 3 ....

....

5 Quantitative Chemistry ⓟ • Grade 8–9 🔲

Copper nitrate solution was electrolysed for 20 minutes with a current of 0.6 A.

0.00024 kg of copper was collected at the cathode.

a) Give the value of the Avogadro constant.   [1 mark]

....

b) Determine the number of atoms produced.   [5 marks]

Give your answer to 3 significant figures.

Relative atomic mass (A_r): Cu = 63.5

....

....

....

....

Total score: .... / 17

Identify

Decide which is the correct name or characteristic from a list.

Example questions

1 Atomic Structure and the Periodic Table P1 • Grade 1–3

The figure below shows part of the Periodic Table. The symbols of the elements have been replaced with letters.

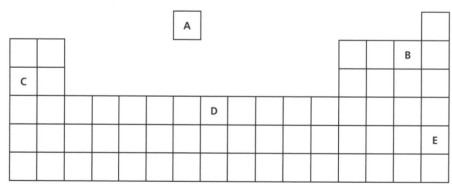

a) Identify an element that has one electron in the outer shell. **[1 mark]**

b) Identify an element that has a full outer shell of electrons. **[1 mark]**

2 Chemical Changes P1 • Grade 8–9

A student put a piece of magnesium metal into a solution of copper(II) nitrate. The balanced symbol equation for this reaction is:

$$Mg(s) + Cu(NO_3)_2(aq) \rightarrow Mg(NO_3)_2(aq) + Cu(s)$$

a) Identify the element being oxidised. **[1 mark]**

b) Identify the ion being reduced. **[1 mark]**

Complete the example

3

The Rate and Extent of Chemical Change P2 • Grade 4–5 🔒

A student wanted to investigate how changes in concentration of hydrochloric acid affect the rates of reaction with sodium thiosulfate. The student used the equipment below.

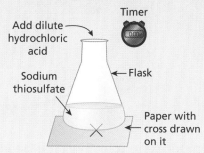

The student added the same volume of hydrochloric acid and sodium thiosulfate to a conical flask and timed how long it took until they could no longer see the cross.

a) Identify the independent variable. [1 mark]

The independent variable is the variable that is changed.

....

b) Identify the dependent variable. [1 mark]

The dependent variable is the variable that you observe and measure during the experiment.

....

Exam practice questions

1 Organic Chemistry P2 • Grade 1–3

This question is about homologous series of organic chemicals. The figure below shows some organic chemicals.

A, B, C, D structures shown.

a) Identify the functional group of **A**. [1 mark]

....

b) Identify the **two** alcohols. [2 marks]

....

c) Identify the substance with a pH lower than 7. [1 mark]

....

2 The Rate and Extent of Chemical Change P2 • Grade 4–5 ⊙

A student wanted to investigate how adding a catalyst to hydrogen peroxide affected the rate of reaction.

The student used the equipment below.

Manganese(IV) oxide (catalyst)

The student added hydrogen peroxide to a conical flask and recorded how much gas was collected every 10 seconds for two minutes.

The student did this experiment twice, once with a catalyst and once without.

a) Identify the dependent variable. **[1 mark]**

....

b) Identify a control variable. **[1 mark]**

....

3 Chemical Changes P1 • Grade 4–5

The photo below shows a sparkler.

Iron metal is used in sparklers. The iron reacts with a gas in the air to make sparks of iron oxide.

a) Identify the gas that iron reacts with. **[1 mark]**

....

b) Identify the type of chemical reaction happening in a lighted sparkler. **[1 mark]**

....

4 Chemical Changes ⓟ • Grade 6–7

This question is about the extraction of copper from its ore.

Malachite is a copper ore containing mainly copper(II) carbonate ($CuCO_3$).

The copper can be extracted in a two-stage process:

Stage 1: $CuCO_3 \rightarrow CuO + CO_2$

Stage 2: $2CuO + C \rightarrow Cu + CO_2$

a) Identify the type of chemical reaction in each stage of the copper extraction.   **[2 marks]**

Stage 1:..

Stage 2:..

b) Identify the substance that is being oxidised in stage 2.   **[1 mark]**

....

5 Chemical Changes ⓟ • Grade 6–7

Iron is extracted from iron ore in the blast furnace.

Coke is an impure form of carbon and reacts with the iron ore to make iron. The equation for this reaction is:

$2Fe_2O_3 + 3C \rightarrow 3CO_2 + 4Fe$

a) Identify the substance that is being reduced.   **[1 mark]**

....

b) A neutralisation reaction is used to remove any acidic waste. Limestone is added to the blast furnace to neutralise acidic gases.

Identify the substance that will react with the limestone.   **[1 mark]**

....

6 Organic Chemistry ⓟ • Grade 8–9

Nettle plants contain an organic acid called formic acid.

A student carefully picked a nettle leaf and crushed it.

Universal indicator was used to test the liquid made from the crushed nettle leaf.

a) Identify the functional group in the formic acid.   **[1 mark]**

....

b) Identify the main hazard in this investigation.   **[1 mark]**

....

Total score:..................... **/ 15**

Name

Only a short answer is required, not an explanation or a description.

Worked examples and more!

TOP TIP
A 'Name' question can often be answered with a single word, phrase or sentence.

Example questions

1 **Chemistry of the Atmosphere P2 • Grade 1–3**

a) Name the gas that mainly makes up dry air. **[1 mark]**

b) Name the process that first produced oxygen in the atmosphere. **[1 mark]**

2 **Chemical Changes P1 • Grade 4–5**

A salt can be made by adding excess copper oxide to sulfuric acid.

The salt solution must be separated from the unreacted copper oxide using the equipment shown.

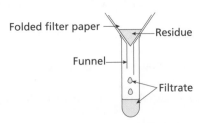

Folded filter paper — Residue
Funnel
Filtrate

a) Name the separating technique shown in the diagram. **[1 mark]**

b) Name the salt that is collected. **[1 mark]**

Complete the example

3 **Atomic Structure and the Periodic Table** **P1** • Grade 1–3

This question is about compounds.

a) Name the compound made when sodium reacts with chlorine. **[1 mark]**

   Sodium

b) Name the elements in the compound lithium bromide. **[2 marks]**

   Lithium and

Exam practice questions

1 **Atomic Structure and the Periodic Table** **P1** • Grade 1–3

This question is about the model of the atom.

a) Name the subatomic particle that has a 1+ charge. **[1 mark]**

b) Name the subatomic particle discovered by James Chadwick. **[1 mark]**

c) Name the scientist who suggested that electrons orbited the nucleus at specific distances. **[1 mark]**

2 **Chemical Analysis** **P2** • Grade 4–5

A solution of iron(II) sulfate contains iron(II) ions and sulfate ions.

Chemical tests can be used to show the presence of each ion.

a) A solution can be added to the iron(II) sulfate to show the presence of iron(II) ions.

   Name the solution added. **[1 mark]**

b) A different solution can be added to the iron(II) sulfate to show the presence of sulfate ions.

   Name the solution added. **[1 mark]**

3   Organic Chemistry ⓟ² / Chemistry of the Atmosphere ⓟ² • Grade 4–5

Natural gas is a fossil fuel and is used in our homes for heating and cooking.

Natural gas is mainly made of an alkane with one carbon atom.

a)   Name the main hydrocarbon found in natural gas.   [1 mark]

....

b)   Name the chemical reaction for when natural gas is used to cook your food.   [1 mark]

....

c)   Name the greenhouse gas that is made when natural gas is used.   [1 mark]

....

4   Chemistry of the Atmosphere ⓟ² • Grade 4–5

Many scientists believe that human activities are causing the mean global temperature of the Earth to increase. They think this is due to an increase in the amounts of greenhouse gases in the atmosphere.

Water vapour is an example of a greenhouse gas.

Name **two** other greenhouse gases.   [2 marks]

....

....

5   Atomic Structure and the Periodic Table ⓟ¹ • Grade 4–5

Early models of atoms showed them as tiny spheres that could not be divided into simpler substances.

In 1897, Thompson discovered that atoms contained small, negatively charged particles. He proposed a new model, shown below.

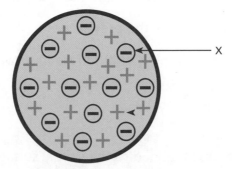

Name the particle labelled X.   [1 mark]

....

6 Bonding, Structure, and the Properties of Matter P1 • Grade 6–7

This question is about the metal sodium and its compounds.

a) Name the bonding in a sample of pure sodium.   [1 mark]

....

b) Name the particle that carries charge in a sample of pure sodium. [1 mark]

....

c) Name the bonding in a pure sample of solid sodium chloride.   [1 mark]

....

d) Name the particle that carries the charge during the electrolysis of
    sodium chloride solution.   [1 mark]

....

7 Organic Chemistry P2 • Grade 8–9

This question is about ethene.

a) Name the **two** processes used to make ethene from crude oil. [1 mark]

....

....

b) Name the **two** products when ethene undergoes complete combustion. [1 mark]

....

....

c) Name the product produced when ethene undergoes an addition
    reaction with steam.   [1 mark]

....

Total score: .... / 18

Write

Recall a fact, definition or equation and write it down. Only a short answer is required, not an explanation or a description.

Worked examples and more!

Example questions

1 Atomic Structure and the Periodic Table P1 • Grade 1–3

Sodium is a Group 1 metal that is stored under oil. The figure on the right is a photograph of sodium metal in storage. When sodium metal is removed from the oil it reacts with oxygen in the air. A white solid of sodium oxide is made.

Write a word equation for this reaction. **[2 marks]**

2 Organic Chemistry P2 • Grade 4–5

Methane is the main hydrocarbon found in natural gas. Natural gas is combusted in gas boilers in homes to provide heat.

Write a word equation for the complete combustion of methane. **[2 marks]**

Complete the example

3   Atomic Structure and the Periodic Table ⓟ1 • Grade 1–3

This question is about displacement reactions of halogens.

Chlorine water was mixed with a solution of potassium bromide.

A chemical reaction happened.

Potassium chloride and bromine were made.

Write a word equation for this reaction. **[2 marks]**

chlorine + _____ → _____ + _____

4   Chemical Analysis ⓟ2 • Grade 8–9

An unknown colourless solution was tested with acidified silver nitrate solution.

The result was a yellow precipitate.

Write an ionic equation to describe this observation.

You do **not** need to include state symbols. **[3 marks]**

Ag^+ + _____ → _____

Exam practice questions

1   Organic Chemistry ⓟ2 • Grade 1–3

Octane is a hydrocarbon found in petrol and can be used to fuel cars.

When octane burns with oxygen from the air, complete combustion takes place.

Write a word equation for the complete combustion of octane. **[2 marks]**

2   Organic Chemistry ⓟ2 • Grade 4–5

Ethanol can be made from fermentation.

This is a sustainable source of ethanol and a type of biofuel.

Ethanol can be added to petrol in car engines.

When ethanol burns in a car engine, complete combustion takes place.

Write a word equation for the complete combustion of ethanol. **[2 marks]**

3 Atomic Structure and the Periodic Table ⓟ • Grade 6–7

Potassium is a Group 1 metal. When a small piece of potassium metal is put into water, it reacts to make potassium hydroxide and a gas.

The figure below shows the reaction.

Write a balanced symbol equation for the reaction between potassium metal and water.

You do **not** need to include state symbols. **[3 marks]**

4 Chemical Changes ⓟ • Grade 8–9 🏠

A student electrolysed a solution of copper(II) chloride.

The figure below is a diagram of the equipment that they used.

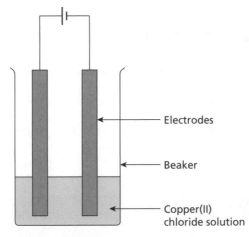

Electrodes

Beaker

Copper(II) chloride solution

a) Write a half equation for the reaction at the anode. **[3 marks]**

b) Write a half equation for the reaction at the cathode. **[3 marks]**

The figure below is a simplified diagram of a hydrogen fuel cell.

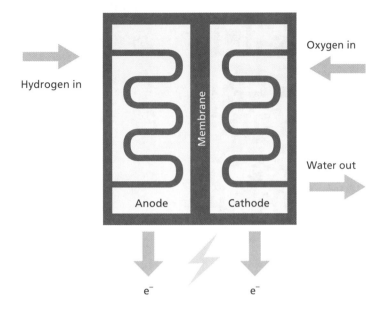

Hydrogen fuel cells offer a potential alternative to rechargeable cells and batteries.

Hydrogen fuel is oxidised to produce pure water.

a) Write a half equation for the reaction at the anode.

You do **not** need to include state symbols. **[3 marks]**

b) Write a half equation for the reaction at the cathode.

You do **not** need to include state symbols. **[3 marks]**

Total score: .... **/ 19**

Worked examples and more!

Complete

Write your answer in the space provided, for example on a diagram, in the gaps in a sentence or in a table.

Example questions

1 Atomic Structure and the Periodic Table P1 • Grade 1–3

Complete the table about subatomic particles. **[3 marks]**

Particle	Relative mass	Relative charge
Proton		1+
	1	0
Electron	0	

2 Organic Chemistry P2 • Grade 4–5

The figure on the right is a diagram of an organic molecule.

Complete the molecular formula for the molecule. **[1 mark]**

Molecular formula = C............ H............

$$
\begin{array}{c}
H \\
H-C-H \\
H \quad | \quad H \\
H-C-C-C-H \\
H \quad | \quad H \\
H-C-H \\
H
\end{array}
$$

Complete the example

3 Chemical Changes P1 • Grade 1–3

This question is about oxidation of reactive metals.

When magnesium is put into a flame it will react with oxygen in the air.

Complete the word equation for this reaction.   **[2 marks]**

magnesium + ... *oxygen* .... → ....

4 Chemical Analysis P2 • Grade 4–5

Complete the sentence.   **[1 mark]**

Chromatography can be used to separate mixtures and can give information to

help identify ....

Exam practice questions

1 Chemistry of the Atmosphere P2 • Grade 1–3

Photosynthesis by algae reduced the percentage of carbon dioxide gas in Earth's early atmosphere.

The percentage of another gas was increased.

Complete the word equation for photosynthesis.   **[2 marks]**

.... + water → glucose + ...

2 Chemical Analysis P2 • Grade 1–3

A simple laboratory test for carbon dioxide is that limewater turns cloudy.

This is a chemical reaction where acidic carbon dioxide gas reacts with an alkali solution of calcium hydroxide.

A white precipitate of calcium carbonate is made.

Complete the balanced symbol equation by adding state symbols.   **[4 marks]**

CO_2 .... + $Ca(OH)_2$ .... → $CaCO_3$ .... + H_2O ....

3   Bonding, Structure, and the Properties of Matter P1 • Grade 1–3

Nitrogen and hydrogen form ammonia.

A hydrogen atom contains one electron.

A nitrogen atom contains five electrons in the outer shell.

Complete the dot-and-cross diagram for a molecule of ammonia.

Show the outer electrons only.

[3 marks]

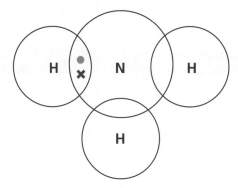

4   Organic Chemistry P2 • Grade 4–5

This question is about combustion.

Complete the sentences.

[3 marks]

a)   Hydrocarbon fuels are combusted to release ....

b)   Incomplete combustion happens when there is limited ....

c)   Alkenes are more likely to undergo ....

5   Energy Changes P1 • Grade 4–5

This question is about energy changes.

Complete the sentences.

[3 marks]

An exothermic reaction is one that transfers energy to the ....

Endothermic reactions cause the temperature of the surroundings to ....

Hand warmers and self-heating cans are examples of everyday uses of ....

....

6 **Bonding, Structure, and Properties of Matter** ⓟ • Grade 4–5

Magnesium is a metal and can form a compound with oxygen.

A magnesium atom contains two electrons in the outer shell.

An oxygen atom contains six electrons in the outer shell.

Complete the dot-and-cross diagram for the compound of magnesium oxide. Show the outer electrons only. **[4 marks]**

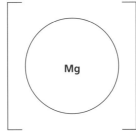 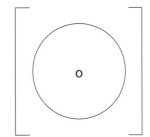

7 **The Rate and Extent of Chemical Change** ⓟ • Grade 4–5 ⓐ

A student wanted to investigate the reaction between magnesium and hydrochloric acid.

The student used the equipment shown in the figure below.

The student investigated different concentrations of hydrochloric acid and measured the mass change to determine the rate of reaction with magnesium metal.

a) Complete the word equation for this reaction. **[2 marks]**

magnesium + hydrochloric acid → .... + ...

b) Complete the sentences. **[2 marks]**

The independent variable is ....

The dependent variable is ....

8   Chemical Changes P1 • Grade 6–7

A student wanted to investigate the electrolysis of sodium chloride solution.

The student used the equipment shown in the figure below.

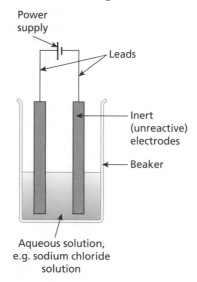

Power supply

Leads

Inert (unreactive) electrodes

Beaker

Aqueous solution, e.g. sodium chloride solution

Complete the sentences.   **[3 marks]**

a)   At the anode, chloride ions are ....

b)   At the cathode, hydrogen ions are ....

c)   The electrolyte can only conduct electricity when the ions are

....

9   Quantitative Chemistry P1 • Grade 6–7

This question is about the amount of substance.

Complete the sentences.   **[2 marks]**

a)   Chemical amounts are measured in ....

b)   The number of atoms, molecules or ions in a mole of a given substance is the

....

10   Atomic Structure and the Periodic Table P1 • Grade 6–7

This question is about halogen displacement reactions.

A student investigated the reactivity of the halogens.

The student mixed chlorine water with potassium bromide solution in a test tube.

a)   Complete the sentence.   **[1 mark]**

A more reactive halogen can displace a less reactive halogen from an aqueous solution

of its ....

b)   Complete the ionic equation for this reaction.   **[2 marks]**

$2Br^-$ + ... → $2Cl^-$ + ...

11 Bonding, Structure, and the Properties of Matter P1 / Organic Chemistry P2 • Grade 8–9

Acetylene is an unsaturated hydrocarbon that contains two carbon atoms and only two hydrogen atoms.

Complete the dot-and-cross diagram for a molecule of acetylene.

Show the outer electrons only.

[2 marks]

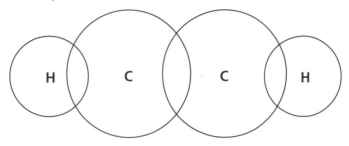

12 Using Resources P2 • Grade 8–9

The Haber process is used to make ammonia.

The diagram below shows an outline of the process.

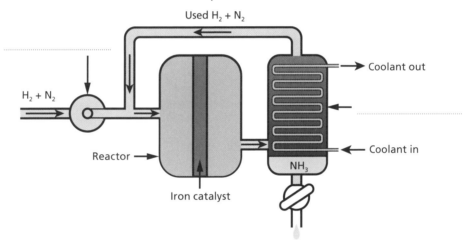

a) Complete the labels on the diagram. **[2 marks]**

b) Complete the balanced symbol equation for the Haber process.

Include state symbols. **[3 marks]**

$$\text{.................... } H_2 \text{ (g) + ... } \rightleftharpoons 2NH_3 \text{ (g)}$$

Total score: .... **/ 38**

Define

Give the exact meaning of a term or idea.

> **TOP TIP**
> Defining something means being very clear about what that thing is.

Example questions

1 **Atomic Structure and the Periodic Table P1 • Grade 1–3**

All substances are made of atoms.

Define an atom. [1 mark]

2 **Organic Chemistry P2 • Grade 4–5**

Methane is an example of a hydrocarbon and the first member of the alkane homologous series. The figure below is a diagram of a molecule of methane. Carbon is shown as black spheres and hydrogen is shown as white spheres.

Define hydrocarbon. [2 marks]

Complete the example

3 Chemical Analysis ② • Grade 4–5

This question is about pure water.

In chemistry, distilled water is pure water but bottled spring water is not.

In everyday language, distilled water and mineral water are both examples of pure water.

a) Define **pure** in terms of chemistry.   [1 mark]

  A single

b) Define **pure** in terms of everyday language.   [1 mark]

  A substance that has had

4 Chemical Changes ① • Grade 6–7

The thermite reaction is used to weld railway tracks together.

Iron oxide is reduced by aluminium in a displacement reaction.

The balanced symbol equation for the reaction is:

$Fe_2O_3 + 2Al \rightarrow Al_2O_3 + 2Fe$

a) Define **oxidation.**   [2 marks]

  Gain of   and loss of

b) Define **reduction.**   [2 marks]

  Loss of   and gain of

Exam practice questions

1 Chemistry of the Atmosphere P2 • Grade 1–3

The average carbon footprint in the UK is about 5000 kg CO_2e per person per year.

Define **carbon footprint**. [2 marks]

2 Energy Changes P1 • Grade 4–5

Hydrocarbon fuels undergo combustion reactions when they are used.

Usually a spark or flame will provide the activation energy to start the combustion reaction.

a) Define **exothermic**. [2 marks]

b) Define **activation energy**. [1 mark]

3 Chemistry of the Atmosphere P2 • Grade 4–5

In the UK, potable water is produced from an unpolluted source of fresh water. Potable water contains low levels of dissolved substances.

Define **potable water**. [1 mark]

4 Quantitative Chemistry P1 / Chemical Changes P1 • Grade 6–7

A student wanted to make a pure dry sample of copper(II) sulfate.

This is the method used:

1. React excess copper(II) oxide with sulfuric acid.

2. Filter off and crystallise the product from the filtrate.

3. Remove the crystals and dry with absorbent paper.

Sulfuric acid was the limiting reactant.

Define **limiting reactant**. [1 mark]

5   Chemical Changes ⓟ • Grade 6–7

Malachite is a copper ore that contains mainly copper(II) carbonate.

Copper compounds can be made into electrolytes. Electrolytes can be reduced to make pure copper.

Define **electrolyte**.   [3 marks]

....

....

....

6   Chemical Changes ⓟ • Grade 8–9 🙂

A student used titration to accurately calculate the concentration of a sample of hydrochloric acid.

The student used the equipment shown in the diagram.

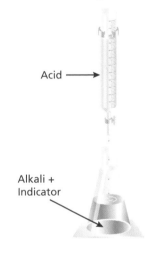

Acid ⟶

Alkali +
Indicator

The student's results were shown to be accurate, repeatable and reproducible.

a)   Define **accurate**.   [1 mark]

....

b)   Define **repeatable**.   [1 mark]

....

....

c)   Define **reproducible**.   [1 mark]

....

....

....

Total score: .... / 13

Describe

You need to give the details of facts or processes in an organised way.

Example questions

1 Chemical Changes P1 • Grade 1–3 🏠

A student carries out a titration to find the volume of hydrochloric acid that reacts with 25 cm³ of sodium hydroxide solution. The diagram shows the equipment used.

Describe how a student could use this equipment to complete the titration. **[5 marks]**

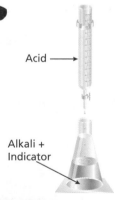

Acid →

Alkali + Indicator

2 Atomic Structure and the Periodic Table P1 • Grade 4–5

The model of the atom has changed over time as new scientific evidence has been collected. In 1897, J.J. Thomson discovered the electron.

Describe the atomic model of the atom that J.J. Thomson proposed. **[2 marks]**

Complete the example

3 Atomic Structure and the Periodic Table P1 • Grade 1–3

This question is about separating mixtures. Sand and water can be mixed together and separated by physical means.

Describe how to obtain a sample of pure dry sand from sandy water.　　　**[3 marks]**

_____ the mixture .

Collect the _____ in the _____ .

Dry the residue by _____ .

4 Chemical Changes P1 / Chemical Analysis P2 • Grade 4–5

A student wanted to investigate the reaction between zinc metal and hydrochloric acid. The student placed a piece of zinc metal into a half-filled test tube of dilute hydrochloric acid.

a) Describe the observations that the student would make.　　　**[2 marks]**

The student would _____

and the zinc would _____ .

b) Describe a simple chemical test to show that one product of the reaction was hydrogen gas.　　　**[2 marks]**

Use a _____ splint .

If the gas is hydrogen, you will hear a _____ .

5 Chemical Changes P1 • Grade 8–9

The label has fallen off a bottle of acid in a laboratory. The acid can only be hydrochloric acid or methanoic acid. Hydrochloric acid is a strong acid. Methanoic acid is a weak acid.

Describe how universal indicator could be used to determine which acid was present in the bottle.　　　**[4 marks]**

This is an AO2 question where you are applying your knowledge of using universal indicator to obtain a pH value. This question includes quality of written communication marks and you need to carefully construct your answer to get a high mark.

Take a small sample of the acid and add _____ to it

or put a drop of the unknown acid on _____ .

Compare the colour of the _____ to the colour chart to

determine the _____ . If the _____ is less than 3 then the acid

is _____ acid. If the _____ is greater than 4 but less

than 7 then the acid is _____ acid .

Exam practice questions

1 Chemical Analysis P2 • Grade 1–3

A student wanted to use chromatography to investigate a food colouring.

The figure below shows how the chromatogram was produced.

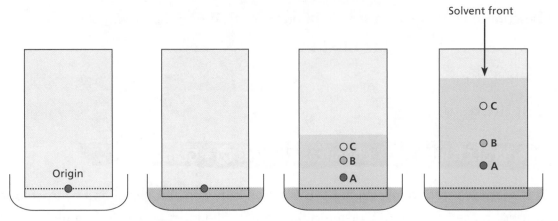

Describe what the chromatogram shows. **[2 marks]**

....

....

....

2 Bonding, Structure, and the Properties of Matter P1 • Grade 1–3

The diagram shows how sodium and chlorine atoms form sodium chloride.

Only the outer electrons are shown.

The dots (•) and crosses (×) are used to represent electrons.

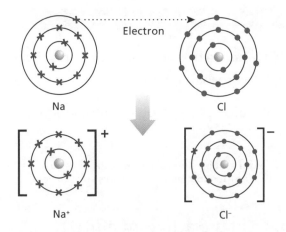

Describe, as fully as you can, what happens when sodium reacts with chlorine to make sodium chloride. **[4 marks]**

....

....

....

....

....

3   Atomic Structure and the Periodic Table ⓟ • Grade 4–5

This question is about the Periodic Table.

a)   Describe how elements were ordered before subatomic particles were discovered.   **[1 mark]**

....

b)   Describe how Mendeleev's Periodic Table was different to the earlier attempts to order elements.   **[2 marks]**

....

....

....

c)   Describe how the modern Periodic Table is different to Mendeleev's original.   **[3 marks]**

....

....

....

4   Chemical Changes ⓟ / Chemical Analysis ⓟ② • Grade 4–5 ⓐ

A student used electrolysis to investigate the products at the electrodes.

The student used the equipment shown in the diagram.

The gaseous products were collected.

In the investigation, samples of chlorine, hydrogen and oxygen gas were collected.

Describe how to test for each gas.   **[6 marks]**

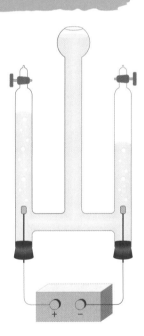

Chlorine: ....

....

Hydrogen: ....

....

Oxygen: ....

....

5. Organic Chemistry ② • Grade 6–7

The fractional distillation of crude oil produces more longer-chain hydrocarbons than needed to meet demand.

Cracking is the process where large hydrocarbons can be broken down to produce smaller, more useful molecules.

a) Catalytic cracking is used to make more shorter-chain alkanes which can be used as fuels in cars.

Describe the conditions for catalytic cracking. **[2 marks]**

b) Steam cracking is used to make alkenes which can be used in polymer production.

Describe the conditions for steam cracking. **[2 marks]**

6. Bonding, Structure, and the Properties of Matter ① • Grade 6–7

Silica is also called silicon dioxide (SiO_2). The figure is a diagram of a crystal of silica.

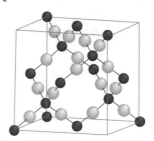

Describe the structure and bonding of silica. **[4 marks]**

7. Using Resources ② • Grade 6–7

Malachite is a copper ore that is becoming scarce.

Bioleaching is a new way of extracting copper from low-grade ores.

Describe how copper is extracted from low-grade ores by bioleaching. **[4 marks]**

8 Bonding, Structure, and the Properties of Matter (P1) • Grade 6–7

A scientific study was carried out during which 10 volunteers applied sunscreen containing zinc oxide nanoparticles twice a day.

After 5 days, less than 0.01% of the nanoparticles had entered the bloodstream. The scientists concluded that there is no danger from zinc oxide nanoparticles in sunscreen.

Describe what extra information you would need to know before you can decide if there is a danger from zinc oxide nanoparticles in the sunscreen. **[3 marks]**

....

....

....

....

9 Bonding, Structure, and the Properties of Matter (P1) / Chemical Changes (P1) • Grade 8–9

Aluminium chloride is an ionic compound that can be made from its elements.

In the industrial manufacture of aluminium chloride, aluminium metal is heated to at least 650°C in an atmosphere of chlorine gas.

Describe, as fully as you can, how this reaction can be classified as a REDOX reaction. **[5 marks]**

....

....

....

....

....

....

Total score: .... **/ 38**

Why/What/Which...

Why/What/Which/ Where/When/Who/How: These command words are used for direct questions to prompt short and precise answers.

TOP TIP
Even though a good answer may be quite brief, it does need to be relevant.

Example questions

1 Chemistry of the Atmosphere P2 • Grade 1–3

a) **When** was the Earth formed? Tick (✔) **one** box. **[1 mark]**

200 million years ago ☐ 200 billion years ago ☐ 4.6 billion years ago ☐

b) The percentage of oxygen increased about 2.7 billion years ago.

Which process caused this increase? Tick (✔) **one** box. **[1 mark]**

Combustion of fossil fuels ☐ Photosynthesis ☐ Volcanic activity ☐

2 Atomic Structure and the Periodic Table P1 / Chemical Analysis P2 • Grade 4–5

Calcium is an element in Group 2 and Period 4 of the Periodic Table.

a) **Which** type of bonding is in pure calcium? Tick (✔) **one** box. **[1 mark]**

Ionic ☐ Metallic ☐ Covalent ☐ Intermolecular forces ☐

b) A flame test can be used to show the presence of calcium ions.

What flame colour is produced by a calcium salt solution? **[1 mark]**

Complete the example

3 Bonding, Structure, and the Properties of Matter P1 / Using Resources P2 • Grade 4–5

Pure iron and steel can rust. The diagram shows the difference in the structure between iron and steel.

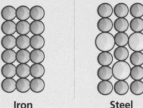

Iron   Steel

a) Which of the following words describe steel?

Tick (✓) **two** boxes.   [2 marks]

> This is an AO2 question as you are asked to remember the definition of the key words and apply it to the example you are being given. Note that you are being asked to tick **two** boxes; there will be 1 mark for each correct answer.

Compound ☐   Formulation ☐

Mixture ☐   Aqueous solution ☐

Element ☐

b) Why are alloys harder than pure metals?   [2 marks]

In pure metals, the layers of _____ easily over each other, but in alloys, the different sizes of _____ distort the layers so they can't _____ as easily .

4 Atomic Structure and the Periodic Table P1 • Grade 6–7

Chlorine has two stable isotopes.

The figure below shows the different symbols for each chlorine isotope.

$$^{35}_{17}Cl \qquad ^{37}_{17}Cl$$

Why is the mass number different for each isotope?   [1 mark]

Each isotope has a different number of _____ .

Exam practice questions

1

This question is about potable water.

In the UK, fresh water is filtered and sterilised to make potable water.

a) What is potable water?

Tick (✓) **one** box. [1 mark]

Rainwater ☐   Pure water ☐   Water that is safe to drink ☐

b) Which is a suitable sterilising agent to use for potable water?

Tick (✓) **one** box. [1 mark]

Oxygen ☐   Chlorine ☐   Carbon dioxide ☐

c) Why is potable water sterilised? [2 marks]

....

....

2

A student wanted to investigate the amount of energy released when metals react with acid.

This was the method used.

1. Measure 20 cm³ of hydrochloric acid into a polystyrene cup.

2. Measure the temperature of the hydrochloric acid.

3. Add 1 g of metal powder to the hydrochloric acid and stir.

4. Measure the highest temperature the mixture reaches.

5. Calculate the temperature increase for the reaction.

6. Repeat steps 1 to 6 with different metals.

a) What type of variable is the type of metal?

Tick (✓) **one** box. [1 mark]

Control ☐   Dependent ☐   Independent ☐

b) What type of variable is the mass of metal used?

Tick (✓) **one** box. [1 mark]

Control ☐   Dependent ☐   Independent ☐

c) What type of variable is the temperature?

Tick (✓) **one** box. [1 mark]

Control ☐   Dependent ☐   Independent ☐

3 Atomic Structure and the Periodic Table P1 • Grade 1–3

This question is about subatomic particles.

a) Who provided evidence to show the existence of neutrons?

Tick (✓) **one** box. **[1 mark]**

Bohr ☐   Chadwick ☐   Mendeleev ☐

b) Where in the atom are neutrons found?

Tick (✓) **one** box. **[1 mark]**

In the nucleus of all atoms ☐

In the nucleus of most atoms ☐

In the atomic energy levels ☐

4 Organic Chemistry P2 / Using Resources P2 • Grade 4–5

Poly(propene) is a polymer used for plastic packaging.

The figure below shows a single-use water bottle made from poly(propene).

WATER

a) What is the name of the monomer used to make poly(propene)? **[1 mark]**

Tick (✓) **one** box.

Propane ☐   Propene ☐   Propanol ☐   Propanoic acid ☐

b) Which chemical reaction is used to make poly(propene) from its monomer?

Tick (✓) **one** box. **[1 mark]**

Condensation polymerisation ☐   Oxidation ☐

Addition polymerisation ☐   Neutralisation ☐

c) How can poly(propene) bottles be recycled into new plastic bottles? **[4 marks]**

....

....

....

....

5 Chemical Changes P1 • Grade 6–7 🏠

A student wanted to make a pure, dry sample of copper(II) chloride.

They used these steps:

1. React an insoluble salt with hydrochloric acid.

2. Filter off the excess.

3. Crystalise the filtrate.

4. Remove crystals and pat dry with absorbent paper.

a) Which of these insoluble solids can be used to make a copper salt by reacting the solid with dilute hydrochloric acid?

Tick (✓) **one** box.   **[1 mark]**

Copper and copper(II) oxide only   ☐

Copper and copper(II) carbonate only   ☐

Copper(II) oxide and copper(II) carbonate only   ☐

Copper, copper oxide and copper carbonate   ☐

b) Often the filtrate is gently heated in the crystalising process.

How should the filtrate be gently heated?   **[1 mark]**

6 Quantitative Chemistry P1 / Chemical Changes P1 / Organic Chemistry P2 • Grade 6–7

This question is about acids.

Hydrogen chloride and methanoic acid both dissolve in water.

All hydrogen chloride molecules ionise in water.

Approximately 4% of methanoic acid molecules ionise in water.

a) What is the molecular formula of methanoic acid?   **[1 mark]**

b) Which of the following best describes a 0.1 g/dm³ solution of methanoic acid?
Tick (✓) **two** boxes.   **[2 marks]**

Has a –COOH functional group   ☐   Is a solution of a strong acid   ☐

Is a concentrated solution   ☐   Has a pH value of more than 7   ☐

Is an aqueous solution   ☐   Is a pure, weak acid   ☐

c) How many moles of methanoic acid are in 1 dm³ of 1 g/dm³ solution of methanoic acid?

Tick (✓) **one** box.   **[1 mark]**

0.02 mol ☐   1 mol ☐   4.6 mol ☐   46 mol ☐

7 The Rate and Extent of Chemical Change (P2) • Grade 6–7 🔒

A student wanted to investigate the rate of reaction between magnesium metal and hydrochloric acid.

The results of the experiment are shown in the graph below.

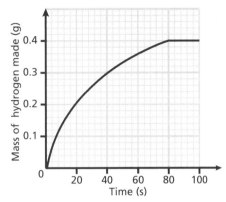

a) What measuring instrument would you use to monitor the dependent variable?　　[1 mark]

....

b) How do the results from the graph above support the conclusion that the reaction stopped at 80 seconds?　　[1 mark]

....

....

8 Chemical Analysis (P2) • Grade 8–9 🔒

This question is about chromatography of inks.

The figure below is a diagram of the equipment used.

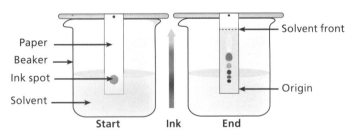

The coloured spots are very close together.

a) Why do the different colours in the ink separate?　　[3 marks]

....

....

....

b) How could the distance between the spots be increased?　　[2 marks]

....

....

Total score: .... / 28

Use

Base your answer on the information provided in the question.

TOP TIP
In some cases, you might be asked to use your own knowledge and understanding.

Example questions

1 Bonding, Structure, and the Properties of Matter **P1** • Grade 1–3

Buckminsterfullerene is made of 60 carbon atoms that are held together by strong bonds. The figure on the right shows a molecule of Buckminsterfullerene.

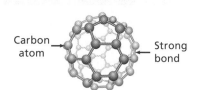

Carbon atom → ← Strong bond

a) What type of structure is Buckminsterfullerene? Tick (✔) **one** box. **[1 mark]**

Use the figure to help you.

Lattice ☐   Molecule ☐   Giant covalent ☐

b) Give the formula of Buckminsterfullerene.

Use the figure to help you. **[2 marks]**

2 Atomic Structure and the Periodic Table **P1** • Grade 4–5

The table gives some information about atoms.

Particle	Atom	Nucleus
Radius (m)	1×10^{-10}	1×10^{-14}

Name the smallest particle.

Use the table. **[1 mark]**

Complete the example

3   Chemistry of the Atmosphere ⓟ2 • Grade 1–3 ▦

The figure below shows the composition of dry air.

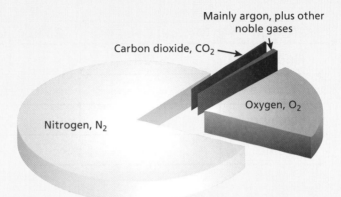

Mainly argon, plus other noble gases

Carbon dioxide, CO_2

Oxygen, O_2

Nitrogen, N_2

a) Name the element that mainly makes up dry air.

Use the figure above.   **[1 mark]**

> Remember that you only need to write the name of the substance, not the formula. However, if you do write the formula, you would still get the mark.

b) Name the group of elements that make up about 1% of dry air.

Use the figure above.   **[1 mark]**

> Groups in the Periodic Table are columns of elements with similar properties.
> You need to know the names of groups 1, 7 and 0. Look carefully at the pie chart: the name of the group is given.

c) Give the fraction of dry air which is made up of oxygen.

Use the figure above.   **[1 mark]**

> Looking at the oxygen slice, you can see that it is about 20% and you need to convert this into a fraction.

Exam practice questions

1 Atomic Structure and the Periodic Table P1 • Grade 1–3 🖩

This question is about halogens. The table shows the melting and boiling points of Group 7 elements.

Element	Melting point (°C)	Boiling point (°C)
Fluorine	−220	−188
Chlorine	−101	−35
Bromine	−7	59
Iodine	114	184

Room temperature is 25°C.

a) Name a halogen that is a gas at room temperature.   **[1 mark]**

Use the table above.

....

b) Describe the trend in melting point.   **[1 mark]**

Use the table above.

....

....

c) Which halogen has the strongest intermolecular forces of attraction?   **[1 mark]**

Use the table above. Tick (✓) **one** box.

Fluorine ☐   Chlorine ☐   Bromine ☐   Iodine ☐

2 Using Resources P2 • Grade 4–5 🖩

This question is about alloys.

a) High carbon steel is an alloy used in construction because it is strong.

The figure below shows a diagram of steel.

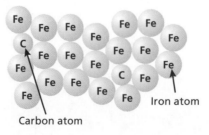

Calculate the ratio of iron to carbon atoms in the sample of steel.

Use the figure above.   **[2 marks]**

....

b)   Bronze is an alloy used to make church bells.

The figure below shows a diagram of bronze.

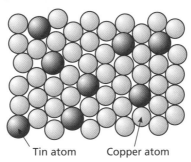

Tin atom   Copper atom

Calculate the percentage of copper atoms in the sample of bronze.

Give your answer to 3 significant figures.

Use the figure above.   **[4 marks]**

....

....

3   **Quantitative Chemistry P1 • Grade 8–9** ▦ ⌂

A student used chromatography to investigate the composition of some fizzy drinks.

The figure below shows the results.

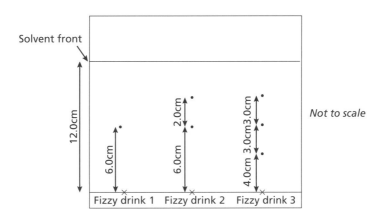

a)   Use the figure above to justify the conclusion that fizzy drink 1 is pure.   **[1 mark]**

....

....

b)   Calculate the R_f value of the common component found in fizzy drinks 1 and 2.

Use the figure above.   **[2 marks]**

....

Total score: .... **/ 12**

Draw

Draw lines to connect information, draw either a complete drawing or diagram or add to one you are given.

TOP TIP
Artistic ability is not important, but clarity and accuracy are. Think about the key features you need to include and ensure that these can be understood.

Example questions

1 Chemistry of the Atmosphere P2 • Grade 1–3

The combustion of fuels causes air pollution.

Draw **one** line from each gas to the environmental problem that it causes.   **[3 marks]**

Methane	Climate change
Sulfur dioxide	Global dimming
Particulates	Acid rain

2 Organic Chemistry P2 • Grade 6–7

Butene is an alkene. Butene can be made from the cracking of long chain hydrocarbons. The figure on the right shows the displayed formula of butene.

$$\begin{array}{c} H \quad\quad H \;\; H \\ \backslash \quad\quad\quad | \;\;\; | \\ C=C-C-C-H \\ / \quad\quad | \;\; | \;\; | \\ H \quad\quad H \;\; H \;\; H \end{array}$$

a) Draw a circle on the figure above to show the alkene functional group. **[1 mark]**

b) Butene will react with bromine water.

Draw the displayed formula of the product of this reaction. **[2 marks]**

Complete the example

3 Atomic Structure and the Periodic Table P1 • Grade 4–5

Magnesium is a Group 2 metal. Chlorine is a Group 7 non-metal. Magnesium and chlorine can react together to make magnesium chloride.

Draw a dot-and-cross diagram to show what happens when atoms of magnesium and chlorine react to produce magnesium chloride. **[5 marks]**

When a metal and a non-metal react together, an ionic compound is formed. Use square brackets to show each individual ion. Remember that metals lose electrons and become positive ions. Non-metals gain electrons and become negative ions.

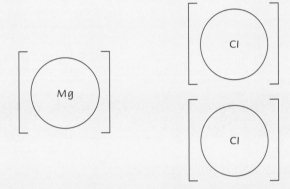

4 Organic Chemistry P2 • Grade 8–9

This question is about synthetic fibres.

The figure below shows a diagram of the repeating unit of the synthetic fibre.

Draw the displayed structural formula of the monomer that is used to make this synthetic fibre. **[3 marks]**

This polymer has only one monomer that is repeated many times to make the polymer. So, this is an example of addition polymerisation and the monomer must be an alkene.

Exam practice questions

1 Chemical Analysis P2 • Grade 1–3 😊

This question is about testing gases.

Draw **one** line from each gas to the test which shows it is present.   **[3 marks]**

Gas		Test
Hydrogen		Glowing splint relights
Carbon dioxide		Damp litmus paper turns white
Oxygen		Burning splint and hear a pop sound
Chlorine		Limewater turns milky

2 Atomic Structure and the Periodic Table P1 / Bonding, Structure, and the Properties of Matter P1 • Grade 4–5

Fluorine is a yellow gas at room temperature.

The proton number of fluorine is 9.

a) Draw the electronic structure of fluorine.   **[2 marks]**

b) Fluorine forms molecules at room temperature.

Draw a dot-and-cross diagram for a fluorine molecule.

Show only the outer shell electrons.   **[2 marks]**

3 Bonding, Structure, and the Properties of Matter ❶ • Grade 6–7

Ionic compounds form between metals and non-metals.

a) Draw the electronic structure of a fluoride ion. Show only the outer shell electrons.

[2 marks]

b) Potassium metal and chlorine gas can react together to make potassium chloride.

Draw the dot and cross diagram of potassium chloride. Show only the outer shell electrons.

[4 marks]

4 Organic Chemistry ❷ • Grade 8–9

Deoxyribonucleic acid is a large molecule essential for life.

The figure below shows a diagram of DNA.

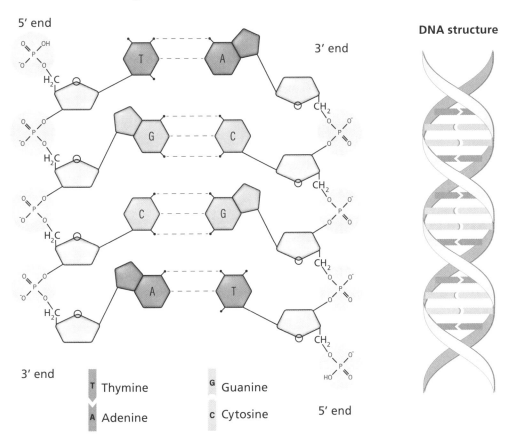

Draw **two** circles around all the nucleotides that contain cytosine.

[2 marks]

Total score: _____ / 15

Sketch

Draw approximately: your drawing doesn't need to be accurate but you should include enough information to demonstrate your understanding of the principles.

Worked example and more!

TOP TIP
The difference between draw and sketch is that more accuracy is expected when drawing whereas sketching involves a degree of approximation.

Example question

1 **The Rate and Extent of Chemical Change** P2 • Grade 4–5 📱 🔒

Rusting is a chemical reaction.
The rate of reaction for the rusting of an iron nail can be monitored by measuring the mass change.

The graph shows the rate of reaction for the rusting of an iron nail.

On the figure, sketch the results you would expect if you used iron powder. **[3 marks]**

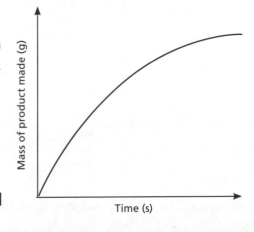

Complete the example

Zinc can react with hydrochloric acid.

Copper powder can be used as a catalyst to increase the rate of reaction.

The figure below shows the energy level diagram for this reaction without a catalyst.

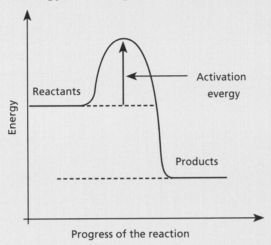

On the figure, sketch the effect of adding a catalyst to this reaction.   **[2 marks]**

Poly(ethene) is a thermosoftening polymer.

By changing the reaction conditions, it is possible to change the structure and therefore the properties.

LD poly(ethene) is softer and more flexible and used for clingfilm.

HD poly(ethene) is rigid and durable and used for shampoo bottles.

Sketch the structure of each form of poly(ethene).   **[3 marks]**

LD poly(ethene)

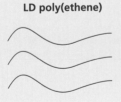

HD polyethene

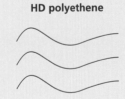

Exam practice questions

1   Using Resources P2 • Grade 1–3

Melamine is a thermosetting plastic.

Sketch the structure of melamine.

Your sketch should include:

•   the polymer chains

•   cross links

[3 marks]

2   The Rate and Extent of Chemical Change P2 • Grade 4–5

A student investigated the volume of gas produced when large lumps of calcium carbonate reacted with hydrochloric acid.

The figure below shows the results of the experiment.

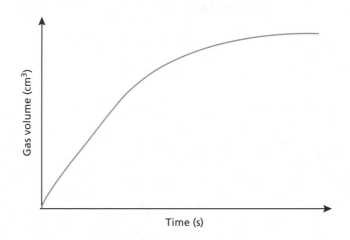

On the figure, sketch the results you would expect if the student doubled the concentration of the acid.

[3 marks]

3

Ethanol can be mixed with petrol and used as a fuel in cars.

Ethanol is combusted in the car engine.

On the figure, sketch the energy level diagram for the combustion of ethanol.　　　**[3 marks]**

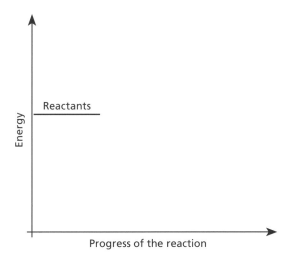

4

Ammonium nitrate is a white solid that dissolves in water.

This change is endothermic.

On the figure, sketch the energy level diagram for this change.　　　**[2 marks]**

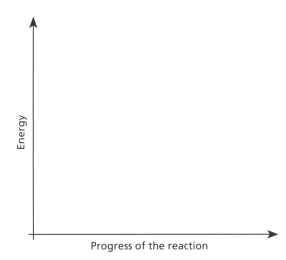

Total score: .... **/ 11**

Label

Add the appropriate names of structures or processes to a diagram.

TOP TIP
Make sure you add clear labels and, where required, clear arrows that show where the labels point.

Example questions

1 **Atomic Structure and the Periodic Table P1 • Grade 1–3**

The figure below is a representation of a sodium atom.

$^{23}_{11}\text{Na}$

Label the atomic number and the mass number on the figure. **[1 mark]**

2 **Energy Changes P1 • Grade 4–5** 🔢

The figure shows the energy level diagram for the combustion of methane.

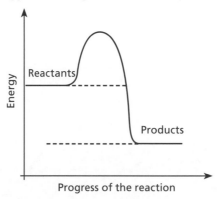

Progress of the reaction

a) **Label** the activation energy on the figure. **[1 mark]**

b) **Label** the overall energy change on the figure. **[1 mark]**

Complete the example

Potable water can be made from the distillation of sea water.

The figure below shows a diagram of the equipment that can be used.

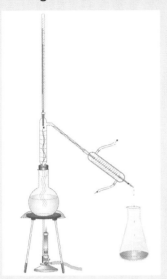

a) Label the piece of equipment that causes the evaporation of sea water. **[1 mark]**

> Evaporation uses energy so you need to think about which part of the diagram is a heating apparatus. Then label it as 'a)' or name the equipment.

b) Label the piece of equipment that causes condensation of the pure water. **[1 mark]**

> The steam needs to be cooled and condensed back to liquid water. Choose the apparatus in the diagram that is cooling and label it as 'b)' or name the equipment.

A student investigated the electrolysis of copper(II) sulfate. The student repeated the experiment using different currents.

The mass of the anode was measured at the start. Each experiment was carried out for five minutes. The anode was then dried and the mass measured again.

The figure below is a graph of the results.

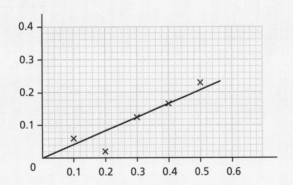

Label the axes. **[4 marks]**

> An independent variable is the variable that you choose to change and is always on the x-axis of the graph. The dependent variable is the variable that you measure in the experiment and is always on the y-axis. The axes labels should have the name of the variable (1 mark each) and the unit that it is measured in (1 mark each).

Exam practice questions

1 Atomic Structure and the Periodic Table P1 • Grade 1–3

Beryllium is a metal element.

The figure below shows the atomic structure of beryllium, including the subatomic particles.

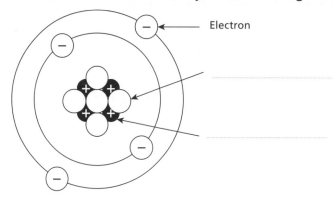

An electron is already labelled.

Label the subatomic particles that are found in the centre of the atom. **[2 marks]**

2 Energy Changes P1 • Grade 4–5 ▣

The reaction of citric acid and sodium hydrogencarbonate is endothermic.

The figure below shows the energy level diagram for the reaction of citric acid with sodium hydrogencarbonate.

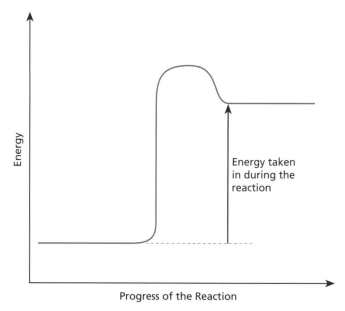

a) Label the reactants and products on the figure. **[1 mark]**

b) Label the activation energy on the figure. **[1 mark]**

3   Chemical Changes ⓟ • Grade 6–7 😊

A student wanted to measure the reacting volumes of a strong acid and a strong alkali.

This is the method used:

1. A known volume of a strong alkali was measured.

2. A suitable indicator was added to the strong alkali.

3. Acid was added until there was a colour change.

4. The volume of acid added was measured and recorded.

The figure below shows equipment set up for a titration.

a) Label the strong acid. [1 mark]

b) Label the strong alkali. [1 mark]

4   Chemistry of the Atmosphere ⓟ • Grade 8–9

Air is the mixture of gases that make up our atmosphere.

The figure below shows the composition of dry air.

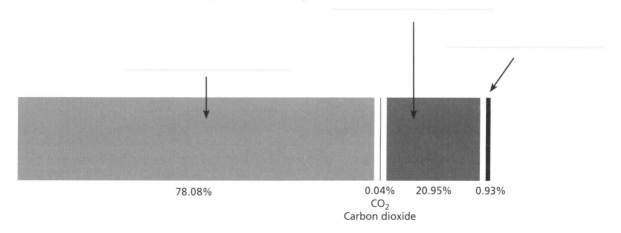

Label the gases on the figure. [3 marks]

Total score: .... / 9

Suggest

Apply your knowledge and understanding to a given situation. Do not expect to have learnt the answer.

Worked examples and more!

Example questions

1 · Using Resources P2 · Grade 1–3

Sea water can be made into potable water by distillation.

Suggest why distilled water is safe to drink. [1 mark]

2 · Chemical Changes P1 · Grade 6–7 ☹

Lead iodide is an insoluble salt that can be made from a reaction between two soluble salts. The equation for the reaction is: $Pb(NO_3)_2 + 2NaI \rightarrow PbI_2 + 2NaNO_3$

Suggest how the lead iodide product could be separated from the mixture at the end of the reaction. [1 mark]

Complete the example

3 Atomic Structure and the Periodic Table ⓟ • Grade 1–3

Iron is a transition metal and can make more than one stable ion. Iron can lose a different number of electrons to become Fe^{2+} or Fe^{3+}

Cobalt is another transition metal that is similar to iron.

Suggest the formula of two stable ions for cobalt.   **[2 marks]**

Co _____ *and* Co _____

4 Energy Changes ⓟ • Grade 8–9 🔢 🏠

A student investigates the energy change of a displacement reaction.

This is the method used:

1. Pour 25 cm³ of copper(II) sulfate solution into a polystyrene cup.
2. Measure the temperature of the copper(II) sulfate solution.
3. Add 2.00 g of zinc powder to the polystyrene cup.
4. Stir the solution.
5. Measure the temperature of the solution every 10 seconds.

The student plotted the results on a graph.

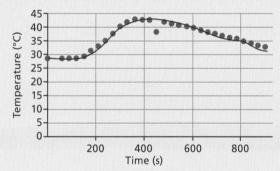

a) Suggest how the colour of the solution would change during the course
    of the reaction.   **[1 mark]**

> Think about what will happen to the blue solution of copper(II) sulfate at the start of the experiment
> and as it is used up to make a colourless solution of zinc sulfate and a precipitate of copper metal.

....

b) Suggest a reason for the anomalous results at 450 s.   **[1 mark]**

> Read the method described in the rubric. Consider if a step could have been missed and if it would
> cause the temperature to be lower than expected.

....

Exam practice questions

1 Using Resources P2 • Grade 1–3

Rings are a type of jewellery and often made of metal.

The picture shows two rings.

a) Suggest **one** reason why pure gold is rarely used for jewellery. **[1 mark]**

b) Suggest **one** way that gold is usually used in jewellery. **[1 mark]**

2 The Rate and Extent of Chemical Change P2 • Grade 4–5

Magnesium reacts with hydrochloric acid to make hydrogen gas and a soluble salt.

A student wanted to investigate how the concentration of acid affected the rate of reaction.

Suggest **two** methods that could be used to monitor the rate of reaction. **[2 marks]**

3 Bonding, Structure, and the Properties of Matter P1 • Grade 6–7

A construction material is made from a compound made between two non-metals. The diagram shows the structure of this material. This material has a very high melting point.

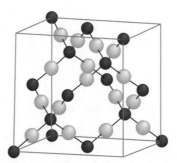

a) Suggest the type of bonding in this material. **[1 mark]**

b) Suggest the structure of this material. **[1 mark]**

4 Chemical Changes ⓟ1 • Grade 6–7 ☻

A student measured the reacting volumes of a strong acid and a strong alkali.

This was the method used:

1. A 25.0 cm³ measuring cylinder was used to transfer 25.0 cm³ of the sodium hydroxide solution into a conical flask.
2. 1 cm³ of methyl orange indicator was added to the sodium hydroxide solution.
3. The burette was filled with 0.1 mol/dm³ hydrochloric acid solution to the 0.00 cm³ mark.
4. The acid was added to the sodium hydroxide solution until the indicator changed colour.
5. The burette was read to find the volume of the solution used.

a) Suggest a more accurate piece of measuring equipment to use in step 1.   **[1 mark]**

....

b) Suggest **two** improvements to step 4 that would increase the accuracy of the results. **[2 marks]**

....

....

c) Suggest **two** units that could be used to measure the concentration of the sodium hydroxide solution.   **[2 marks]**

....

5 Organic Chemistry ⓟ2 / Using Resources ⓟ2 • Grade 8–9

Poly(styrene) is a thermosoftening polymer. Poly(styrene) can solidify as gases are blown through it to make a foam that is often used in packaging.

The figure below shows the structure of poly(styrene).

Polystyrene

a) Suggest why poly(styrene) can be classified as an unsaturated hydrocarbon.   **[2 marks]**

....

....

b) Suggest why poly(styrene) is easier to recycle than most thermosetting polymers.   **[2 marks]**

....

....

....

Total score: .... / 15

Explain

Give reasons for something happening or make the relationships between things clear.

TOP TIP
Your answer may involve several sentences and the words 'because' or 'therefore' are often needed in your answer.

Example question

1 **Bonding, Structure, and the Properties of Matter P1 • Grade 4–5**

Carbon nanotubes are like a rolled-up sheet of graphene. The figure on the right shows a carbon nanotube.

Explain why carbon nanotubes can conduct electricity. **[2 marks]**

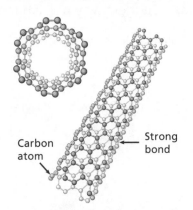

Carbon atom

Strong bond

Complete the example

2   Chemical Analysis **P2** • Grade 1–3

Limewater goes cloudy because insoluble calcium carbonate has been made.

Explain how the calcium carbonate can be separated from the liquid.   **[2 marks]**

_____ the mixture. Collect the _____ in the filter paper.

As calcium carbonate is _____ , this is the solid.

3   Quantitative Chemistry **P1** / The Rate and Extent of Chemical Change **P2** • Grade 7–8

A student investigated the decomposition of copper(II) carbonate.

This was the method used:

1. 1 g of copper(II) carbonate was placed in a boiling tube.
2. The copper(II) carbonate was heated strongly until there was no further visible change.
3. After cooling, the new mass of the product was measured.

The table shows the student's results.

Substance	Mass at start (g)	Mass at end (g)
Copper(II) carbonate	1.00	0.64

Explain the student's results.   **[4 marks]**

In a chemical reaction, no _____ are lost or made. The atoms are

just rearranged and so the mass of the products _____ the mass of

the reactants. But in the decomposition of copper(II) carbonate it looks like

the mass _____ . This is because a _____ is made which

will go into the air. So, the mass of the solid product is _____ than

the mass of the solid reactant and you do not measure the mass of the gas

lost to the _____ .

Exam practice questions

(46)

1   Chemical Changes **P1** • Grade 4–5

When magnesium is put into a blue Bunsen flame a bright white light is observed. A white powder of magnesium oxide is produced.

Explain why this is an example of an oxidation reaction.   **[1 mark]**

2 Atomic Structure and the Periodic Table ⓟ / Bonding, Structure, and the Properties of Matter ⓟ • Grade 4–5

The Periodic Table is a list of all the elements.

Metals are found on the left and towards the bottom of the Periodic Table.

Metals can react with non-metals to make ionic compounds.

a) Explain how metal elements become ions. [2 marks]

....

....

b) Explain how non-metal elements become ions. [2 marks]

....

....

3 Atomic Structure and the Periodic Table ⓟ • Grade 4–5

This question is about groups in the Periodic Table.

a) Explain how the reactivity of Group 1 changes as you go down the group. [4 marks]

....

....

....

....

b) Explain how the reactivity of Group 7 changes as you go down the group. [4 marks]

....

....

....

....

c) Explain why Group 0 is unreactive. [1 mark]

....

....

4 The Rate and Extent of Chemical Change P2 • Grade 4–5

Magnesium metal reacts with hydrochloric acid.

The equation for the reaction is:

magnesium + hydrochloric acid → magnesium chloride + hydrogen

Heating the acid increases the rate of reaction.

Using magnesium powder instead of magnesium ribbon increases the rate of reaction.

a) Explain how increasing the temperature of the acid increases the rate of reaction. **[4 marks]**

....

....

....

....

....

b) Explain how using magnesium powder increases the rate of reaction.   **[3 marks]**

....

....

....

....

5 Chemical Changes P1 • Grade 6–7

Electrolysis can be used to extract aluminium from bauxite ore.

The figure below shows a diagram for the process.

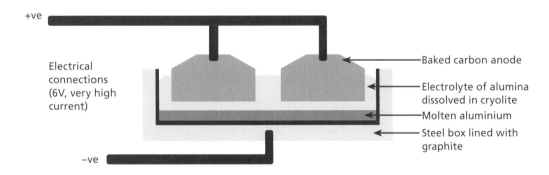

a) Explain why the electrolyte must be molten.   **[2 marks]**

....

....

b) Explain why cryolite is added to the electrolyte. **[2 marks]**

c) Explain why the positive anode must be continually replaced. **[4 marks]**

6 Bonding, Structure, and the Properties of Matter ⓟ • Grade 6–7

Carbon is contained in many different substances.

Diamond and methane both contain carbon.

The figure below shows a diagram of diamond and a diagram of methane.

Diamond	Methane

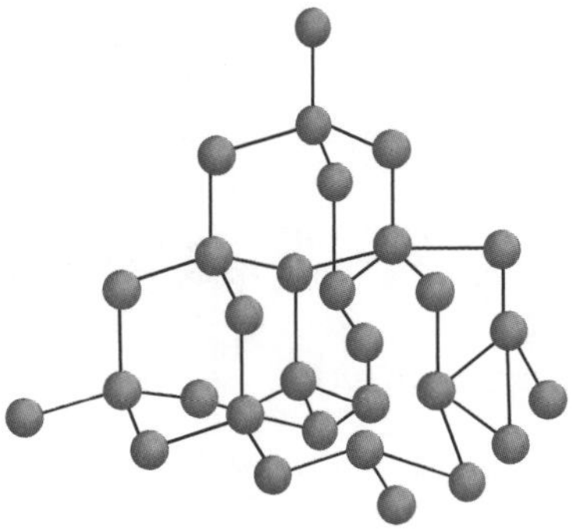

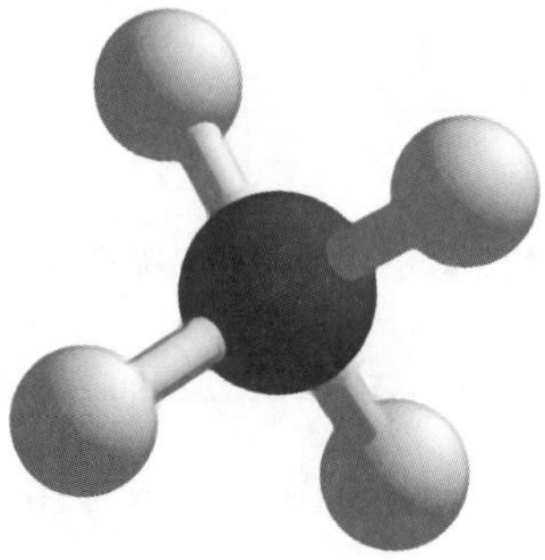

Explain why diamond has a very different melting point to methane. **[6 marks]**

7

Quantitative Chemistry ⓟ / Using Resources ⓟ • Grade 8–9 ▣

Copper ores are becoming scarce and new ways of extracting copper from low-grade ores are being used.

Copper can be obtained from solutions of copper compounds by displacement using scrap iron.

The ionic equation for this reaction is:

$CuSO_4 + Fe \rightarrow FeSO_4 + Cu$

The relative formula mass of $CuSO_4$ is 159 and for $FeSO_4$ is 152.

The relative atomic mass of Fe is 56 and for Cu is 63.5.

A student used 160 g of copper(II) sulfate and 28 g of iron.

Explain which substance is the limiting reactant. **[6 marks]**

8

Quantitative Chemistry ⓟ / Chemical Changes ⓟ • Grade 8–9 ▣

Hydrogen chloride gas can dissolve in water to make hydrochloric acid.

Solution A is made by dissolving 36.5 g of hydrogen chloride gas in 1 dm^3 of pure water.

Solution B is made by dissolving 18.25 g of hydrogen chloride gas in 250 cm^3 of pure water.

a) Explain why hydrochloric acid is a strong acid. **[2 marks]**

b) Explain which solution is the most concentrated. **[3 marks]**

Total score: .... / 46

Show

Provide evidence to reach a conclusion. This usually involves using mathematics to show that a statement or result is correct.

Worked examples and more!

TOP TIP
Make sure you include all the steps leading to the conclusion.

Example questions

1 The Rate and Extent of Chemical Change P2 / Using Resources P2 • Grade 1–3

The Haber process is used to manufacture ammonia. Ammonia is made from its elements in a reversible reaction.

Show this reversible reaction in a word equation. **[2 marks]**

2 Chemical Changes P1 / Quantitative Chemistry P1 • Grade 8–9 ▦

Ethanol can be made by hydration of ethene. The equation for the reaction is:
$C_2H_4 + H_2O \rightarrow C_2H_5OH$

Show that the atom economy is 100%. **[5 marks]**

Complete the example

3   Quantitative Chemistry P1 • Grade 4–5 🔢

A student used electrolysis to extract copper metal from copper(II) sulfate solution.
The student calculated that they could obtain a maximum of 63.5 g of copper.
The student collected 15.8 g.

Show that the student obtained a 25% yield.   **[3 marks]**

$$\text{Percentage yield} = \frac{\text{mass of actual product made}}{\text{maximum theoretical yield of product}} \times 100$$

$$= (\underline{\hspace{1cm}} \div \underline{\hspace{1cm}}) \times 100$$

$$= \underline{\hspace{3cm}}, \text{ which rounds to 25\%}$$

4   Quantitative Chemistry P1 • Grade 6–7 🔢

Sodium hydroxide solid readily dissolves in water to make an aqueous solution.
Two different solutions were made up.
The table shows the concentration of the two solutions.

Solution	Concentration
A	1.00 mol/dm³
B	40 g/dm³

Show that both solutions are the same concentration.   **[4 marks]**

Relative atomic masses (A_r):   H = 1   O = 16   Na = 23

1 mol/dm³ has 1 mole of NaOH per _____ dm³ of solution.

40 g/dm³ has _____ g of NaOH per 1 dm³ of solution.

M_r of NaOH = _____ = _____

1 mole of NaOH has a mass of _____ g

Exam practice questions

1   Chemistry of the Atmosphere P2 • Grade 1–3

The proportions of different gases in the Earth's atmosphere have been the same for about 200 million years. There is 80% nitrogen and the rest is oxygen.

Show that the ratio of nitrogen to oxygen is 4 : 1   **[3 marks]**

....

....

2   The Rate and Extent of Chemical Change P2 • Grade 1–3

Ammonium chloride undergoes thermal decomposition to make ammonia and hydrogen chloride gas.

Show this reversible reaction in a word equation.   **[1 mark]**

3   Quantitative Chemistry P1 / Chemical Changes P1 • Grade 4–5 ▦

Zinc carbonate can undergo thermal decomposition.

The equation for the reaction is:

$ZnCO_3 \rightarrow ZnO + CO_2$

125 g of zinc carbonate was used and the reaction was completed.

Show that 44 g of carbon dioxide was released.

Relative atomic masses (A_r):   C = 12   O = 16   Zn = 65   **[2 marks]**

4   Quantitative Chemistry P1 / Chemical Changes P1 • Grade 6–7 ▦

The thermite reaction is used to weld railway tracks together. The figure below shows a diagram of the process.

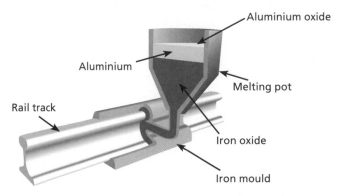

The equation for the reaction is:

$2Al + Fe_2O_3 \rightarrow 2Fe + Al_2O_3$

A mixture of 0.5 kg of aluminium with 1.5 kg of iron(II) oxide was used.

Show that aluminium is the limiting reagent.

Relative atomic masses (A_r):   O = 16   Al = 27   Fe = 56   **[5 marks]**

5 Chemical Analysis P2 • Grade 8–9

A student investigated the composition of a pure white solid. The student found that the compound readily dissolved in water.

The solution of the compound had no effect on flame colour.

The solution formed a white precipitate with excess sodium hydroxide solution.

The solution also formed a white precipitate with acidified silver nitrate.

Show that the compound is magnesium chloride.   **[4 marks]**

6 Organic Chemistry P2 • Grade 8–9

Decolourising of bromine water is a simple laboratory test to show that an unsaturated compound is present.

Ethene is an unsaturated hydrocarbon.

The figure below shows the displayed formula of an ethene molecule and a bromine molecule.

Ethene   **Bromine**

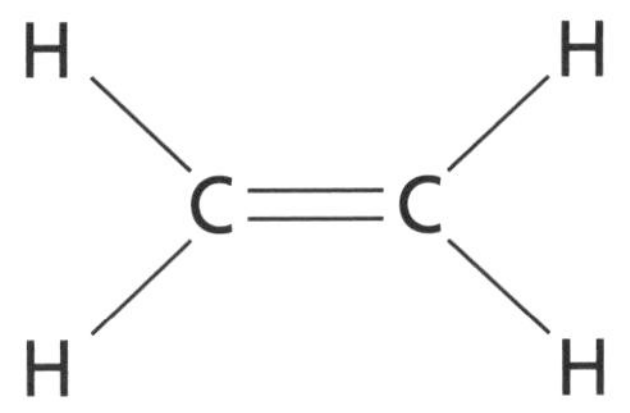

$$H_2C = CH_2$$

Br – Br

Show that the product of this simple laboratory test with ethene would be a saturated compound.   **[3 marks]**

Total score: .... / 18

Determine

Use the given data or information to obtain your answer.

Worked examples and more!

> **TOP TIP**
> The data might be from a graph or table.

Example questions

1 Organic Chemistry P2 • Grade 1–3

Crude oil is a mixture of hydrocarbons. Crude oil is made mainly of alkanes. The table shows the names and formula of the alkanes found in crude oil.

Name	Methane	Ethane	Propane
Formula	CH_4	C_2H_6	C_3H_8

Determine the general formula for alkanes. **[1 mark]**

2 Chemical Analysis P2 • Grade 8–9 🖩 ☺

A student used chromatography to analyse the colouring in fizzy drinks. The figure shows the chromatogram the student produced.

Determine the R_f value of the colouring that was common to fizzy drinks 1 and 2. **[3 marks]**

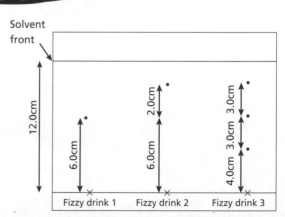

Complete the example

3 The Rate and Extent of Chemical Change P2 • Grade 4–5 🔢 🏠

A student monitored the rate of reaction between hydrochloric acid and magnesium ribbon. The figure below is a graph of the results.

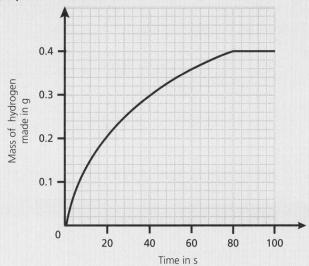

a) Determine the mean rate of reaction in the first 20 seconds. **[3 marks]**

Mean rate of reaction = change in mass ÷ ....

= .... ÷ 20 = ...

b) Determine when the reaction stopped. **[2 marks]**

.... seconds

4 Organic Chemistry P2 • Grade 6–7 🔢

Cycloalkanes are ring-shaped, saturated hydrocarbon molecules. The table shows the names and formula of cycloalkanes.

Name	Formula
Cyclopentane	C_5H_{10}
Cyclohexane	C_6H_{12}
Cycloheptane	C_7H_{14}

a) Determine the general formula for cycloalkanes. **[1 mark]**

C .... H ....

b) Determine the displayed structural formula for cyclobutene. **[3 marks]**

Use the rubric: you know that a closed ring needs to be made. Remember what 'but' means in terms of the number of carbon items in cyclo**but**ene.

C —— C

Exam practice questions

1 Bonding, Structure, and the Properties of Matter P1 • Grade 1–3 🔢

Nanoparticles are smaller than fine particles.

Fine particles have diameters between 100 nm and 2500 nm.

The figure shows a diagram of a nanoparticle.

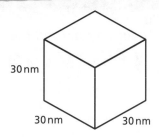

Determine the volume of this nanoparticle. **[3 marks]**

....

....

Volume = ...

2 Energy Changes P1 • Grade 4–5 🏠

A student investigates the reactivity of metals with nitric acid.

This is the method used:

1. Measure 20 cm³ of nitric acid into a polystyrene cup.
2. Measure the temperature of the nitric acid.
3. Add one spatula of metal powder to the nitric acid and stir.
4. Measure the highest temperature the mixture reaches.
5. Calculate the temperature increase for the reaction.
6. Repeat steps 1 to 5 three more times and take an average.
7. Repeat steps 1 to 6 with different metals.

The table shows the results of the experiment.

Metal	Temperature increase in °C				Mean temperature increase in °C
	Trial 1	Trial 2	Trial 3	Trial 4	
Cobalt	6	7	5	9	7
Calcium	54	50	53	55	53
Copper	0	0	0	0	0

a) Determine the independent variable in this experiment. **[1 mark]**

....

b) Determine the unit of the dependent variable in this experiment. **[1 mark]**

....

c) Determine the order of reactivity for the metals cobalt, calcium and copper. **[1 mark]**

most reactive ....

....

least reactive ....

3 Chemistry of the Atmosphere ⒫2 / Quantitative Chemistry ⒫1 • Grade 6–7 📱 🔒

A teacher investigated the reaction of iron with oxygen. The reaction went to completion and there were no limiting reactants.

The word equation for the reaction is:

iron + oxygen → iron oxide

The teacher measured the mass of:

- the glass tube

- the glass tube and iron before the reaction

- the glass tube and iron oxide after the reaction.

The table shows the teacher's results.

	Mass in g
Glass tube	50.00
Glass tube and iron	106.00
Glass tube and iron oxide	130.00

Determine the balanced equation for the reaction.

Relative atomic masses (A_r):   O = 16   Fe = 56   **[6 marks]**

....

....

....

....

....

4 Quantitative Chemistry ⒫1 / Chemical Changes ⒫1 • Grade 8–9 📱

Sulfuric acid can be neutralised by potassium hydroxide.

The balanced symbol equation for this reaction is:

$H_2SO_4 + 2KOH \rightarrow K_2SO_4 + 2H_2O$

Determine the volume of 0.12 mol/dm³ potassium hydroxide that would be needed to fully neutralise 10.0 cm³ of 0.05 mol/dm³ sulfuric acid.   **[5 marks]**

....

....

....

....

....

Volume of potassium hydroxide = ... cm³

Total score: .... / 17

Balance

Balance a chemical equation.

Worked examples and more!

TOP TIP
Remember there are the same number and type of atoms at the start of the reaction as at the end of the reaction.

Example questions

1 **Organic Chemistry P2 • Grade 1–3** 🔲

Alkanes can be used as fuels.

Balance the equation for the complete combustion of methane. **[1 mark]**

$$CH_4 + \rule{1cm}{0.4pt} O_2 \rightarrow CO_2 + 2H_2O$$

2 **Atomic Structure and the Periodic Table P1 • Grade 7–8** 🔲

A student investigated the displacement reaction between potassium iodide solution and chlorine water.

Balance the ionic equation for this reaction. **[1 mark]**

$$\rule{1cm}{0.4pt} I^- (aq) + \rule{1cm}{0.4pt} Cl_2 (aq) \rightarrow \rule{1cm}{0.4pt} Cl^- (aq) + \rule{1cm}{0.4pt} I_2 (aq)$$

Complete the example

3 Using Resources P2 • Grade 4–5 🖩

The Haber process is used to manufacture ammonia. Ammonia can be used to make nitrogen-based fertilisers.

Balance the equation for the Haber process.

$N_2 + 3H_2 \rightleftharpoons$ .... NH_3 .... **[1 mark]**

4 Chemical Changes P1 • Grade 8–9 🖩 😧

A student investigated the electrolysis of copper sulfate solution.

Balance the half equation for the reaction at the cathode.

$4OH^- \rightarrow O_2 +$ .... $H_2O +$ .... e^- **[2 marks]**

Exam practice questions

1 Atomic Structure and the Periodic Table P1 • Grade 1–3 🖩

Group 1 metals react easily with oxygen.

Balance the equation for the oxidation of lithium.

.... $Li + O_2 \rightarrow$ .... Li_2O **[1 mark]**

2 Organic Chemistry P2 • Grade 4–5 🖩

Ethanol can be used as a fuel.

Balance the symbol equation for the complete combustion of ethanol.

$C_2H_5OH +$ .... $O_2 \rightarrow$ .... $CO_2 +$ .... H_2O **[1 mark]**

3 Chemical Changes P1 • Grade 6–7 🖩 😧

A student investigated the electrolysis of copper(II) chloride solution.

a) Balance the half equation for the reaction at the anode.

.... $Cl^- \rightarrow$ .... $Cl_2 +$ .... e^- **[1 mark]**

b) Balance the half equation for the reaction at the cathode.

.... $Cu^{2+} +$ .... $e^- \rightarrow$ .... Cu **[1 mark]**

Total score: .... **/ 4**

Calculate

Use the number values given in the question to work out the answer.

Worked examples and more!

TOP TIP
You may need to give your answer in standard form, or to a certain number of decimal places or significant figures.

Example questions

1 **Atomic Structure and the Periodic Table P1 • Grade 1–3** 🖩

Sodium is an alkali metal. The figure on the right shows information about one atom of sodium.

Calculate the number of neutrons in one atom of sodium. **[1 mark]**

> 23
> **Na**
> sodium
> 11

2 **Atomic Structure and the Periodic Table P1 • Grade 6–7** 🖩

Chlorine has two stable isotopes.

The table shows the composition of a sample of chlorine gas.

Chlorine isotope	$^{35}_{17}Cl$	$^{37}_{17}Cl$
Composition (%)	75	25

Calculate the relative atomic mass of chlorine. **[2 marks]**

Complete the example

3 Quantitative Chemistry ℗1 • Grade 4–5 🖩

Carbon dioxide, CO_2, is found in small proportions in the air.

Calculate the relative formula mass of carbon dioxide.

Relative atomic masses (A_r):   C = 12   O = 16   **[1 mark]**

12 + (_____ × _____) = _____

4 Quantitative Chemistry ℗1 • Grade 8–9 🖩

Iron can be extracted from the reduction of iron(III) oxide using carbon.

The equation for this reaction is:

$2Fe_2O_3 + 3C \rightarrow 4Fe + 3CO_2$

320 tonnes of iron(III) oxide are put into a blast furnace and 198 tonnes of pure iron are extracted.

Relative atomic masses (A_r):   C = 12   O = 16   Fe = 56

1 tonne = 1000 kg

a) Calculate the percentage composition of iron in iron(III) oxide.   **[3 marks]**

M_r of Fe_2O_3 = (_____ × _____) + (_____ × _____) = _____

% Fe = (_____ × _____) ÷ _____ × 100 = _____ %

b) Calculate the percentage yield of this reaction.   **[6 marks]**

$$\% \text{ yield} = \frac{\text{Mass of product actually made}}{\text{Maximum theoretical mass of product}} \times 100$$

Moles of iron(III) oxide used = $\dfrac{\rule{1.5cm}{0.4pt} \times \rule{1.5cm}{0.4pt} \times \rule{1.5cm}{0.4pt}}{160}$

= _____ moles

Mole ratio iron(III) oxide : iron is 1 : _____

So maximum number of moles of iron that can be made = _____ moles

Theoretical yield = _____ × _____ = _____ g = _____ tonnes

% yield = (_____ ÷ _____) × 100 = _____ %

Exam practice questions

1 Bonding, Structure, and the Properties of Matter P1 • Grade 1–3

Nanoparticles can have different properties to the same materials in bulk.

The figure below is a diagram of a nanoparticle.

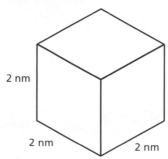

2 nm

2 nm   2 nm

Calculate the volume of this nanoparticle.   **[2 marks]**

...................................nm³

2 The Rate and Extent of Chemical Change P2 • Grade 4–5

A student investigated the rate of reaction between magnesium ribbon and hydrochloric acid.

The figure below shows the equipment used to monitor the reaction.

The starting mass was 404.80 g.

The reaction finished after 90 seconds with the final mass reading 403.65 g.

Calculate the mean rate of reaction.

Give your answer to 3 significant figures. Choose the unit from the box.   **[4 marks]**

g	s/g	g/dm³	mol/dm³	g/s

....

....

3 Quantitative Chemistry P1 / Using Resources P2 • Grade 6–7

Ammonia, NH_3, is made in the Haber process.

Ammonia can be used to make nitrogen-based fertilisers, which are important for reliable food production.

a) Calculate the relative formula mass of ammonia.

Relative atomic masses (A_r):   H = 1   N = 14   **[1 mark]**

....

b) Calculate the percentage composition of nitrogen in one molecule of ammonia.   **[2 marks]**

.... %

4 Quantitative Chemistry P1 • Grade 8–9

A student made a standard solution of hydrochloric acid, HCl.

The student used 1.825 g of hydrochloric acid and 500 cm^3 of pure water.

a) Calculate the number of moles of hydrochloric acid the student used.   **[3 marks]**

.... mol

b) Calculate the concentration of hydrochloric acid in g/dm^3.   **[3 marks]**

.... g/dm^3

c) Calculate the concentration of hydrochloric acid in mol/dm^3.   **[2 marks]**

.... mol/dm^3

Total score:................. / 17

Plan

Write a method for carrying out an investigation. This will usually cover one of the required practicals from the specification.

Worked examples and more!

TOP TIP
The question may give you hints on what to include in your method or give suggested apparatus.

Example questions

1 Using Resources P2 • Grade 1–3

Iron is a transition metal. Iron rusts when it is left open to the air.

Plan an investigation to show that both water and air are needed for iron to rust. Use apparatus and materials from the box. **[6 marks]**

drying agent	iron nails	kettle	oil
stoppers	test tubes and rack	water	

2 Chemical Analysis P2 • Grade 4–5

Red sweets are made attractive using colourings that contain a dye.

Plan an investigation to determine the R_f value for the red dye in this food colouring.

Your plan should include the use of:
- a beaker
- a solvent
- chromatography paper.

[6 marks]

Complete the example

3 Chemical Changes P1 • Grade 4–5 🔒

A student is given three metals, 1, 2 and 3, to identify. The metals are calcium, zinc and silver.

Plan an investigation to identify the three metals by comparing their reactions with dilute nitric acid.

Your plan should give valid results.   **[4 marks]**

Add the same mass and _____ of metals to the same

_____ and concentration of (dilute) nitric acid.

Observe the temperature change or the number of _____ .

Determine conclusion:

- Silver has no reaction.

- Zinc has some bubbles and _____ in temperature.

- Calcium has _____ and the _____

  in temperature.

4 The Rate and Extent of Chemical Change P2 • Grade 6–7 🔢 🔒

Dilute hydrochloric acid can react with sodium thiosulfate solution.

The equation for the reaction is:

$Na_2S_2O_3 (aq) + 2HCl (aq) \rightarrow 2NaCl (aq) + SO_2 (g) + H_2O (l) + S (s)$

Plan an investigation to show how the concentration of the sodium thiosulfate solution affects the rate of the reaction with dilute hydrochloric acid.

Your plan should give valid results.   **[6 marks]**

Put a measured volume of sodium thiosulfate into a _____ .

Add a measured volume of hydrochloric acid.

Immediately put the reaction vessel on a _____ or between

_____ and start a _____ .

Measure the time for the _____ to become no longer

_____ .

Repeat and find the _____ .

Repeat for different _____ of sodium thiosulfate.

Exam practice questions

1 Chemical Analysis P2 • Grade 1–3 ⌂

Some metal ions cause distinctive colours in a flame.

Plan an investigation to use a flame test to show that a solution contains copper ions.

[4 marks]

2 Chemical Changes P1 • Grade 4–5 🔢 ⌂

Plan a method for making pure dry crystals of copper(II) sulfate crystals from copper(II) oxide and dilute sulfuric acid.

In your method you should name the apparatus you will use.

You do not need to mention safety.

[6 marks]

3 Chemical Changes ● • Grade 6–7 😊

A student was investigating the electrolysis of solutions.

They noticed effervescences at the electrodes and collected the gases into test tubes and put a stopper on them.

Plan an investigation to identify the gases that were collected.

You do not need to mention safety. **[6 marks]**

....

....

....

....

....

....

....

....

....

4 Using Resources ● / Quantitative Chemistry ● • Grade 6–7 😊

A student wanted to investigate the concentration of salts in sea water.

Plan an investigation to calculate the concentration of salts in a sample of sea water.

You do not need to mention safety. **[6 marks]**

....

....

....

....

....

....

....

....

....

....

Total score: .... **/ 22**

Plot

Construct a graph on a printed grid using data given in the question.

Worked example and more!

TOP TIP
If you are asked to draw a line of best fit, this could be a smooth curve or one straight line.

Example question

1   **Chemistry of the Atmosphere P2 • Grade 1–3**

Dry air is mainly nitrogen and oxygen.

The table shows the percentages of the two gases in air.

Gas	Percentage (%) composition
Nitrogen	80
Oxygen	20

Plot the percentage of oxygen on the graph.   **[1 mark]**

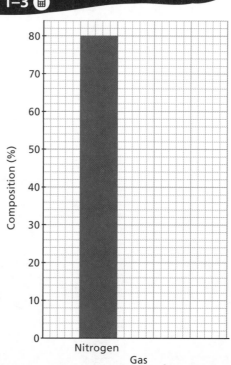

Complete the example

Sodium thiosulfate solution reacts with dilute hydrochloric acid to form a cloudy solution.

A student is investigating how the concentration of sodium thiosulfate affects the rate of reaction. The student uses the equipment shown. The table shows the results.

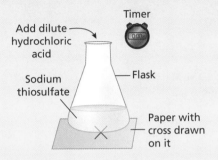

Concentration (arbitrary units)	Time (s)
10	180
20	100
30	70
40	50
50	45
60	40
70	35

Plot the data from the table on the graph below.   **[2 marks]**

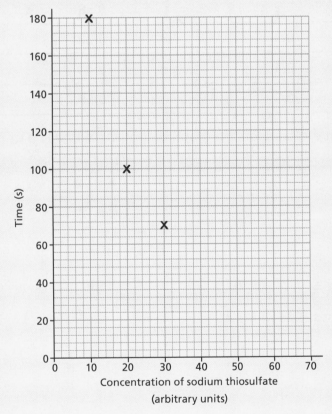

A student is investigating how current affects the mass of the anode in solution electrolysis.

The figure shows the equipment that the student uses.

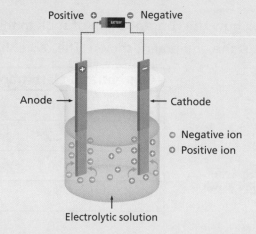

The table shows the student's results.

Current (A)	Change in mass of the anode (g)
0.1	0.06
0.2	0.58
0.3	0.32
0.4	0.44
0.5	0.58

Plot the data from the table on the graph below and add a line of best fit.   **[2 marks]**

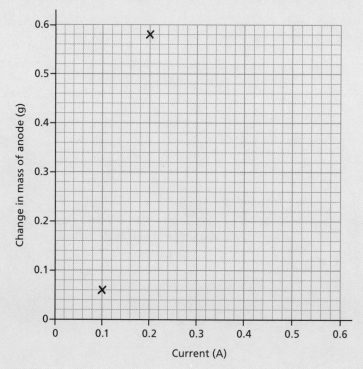

Exam practice questions

Gold used as jewellery is usually an alloy with silver, copper and zinc.

The proportion of gold in the alloy is measured in carats.

The table shows the percentage of gold in different alloys.

Carat	Percentage of gold (%)
24	100
18	75

Plot the percentage of gold in 18-carat gold on the graph below.   **[1 mark]**

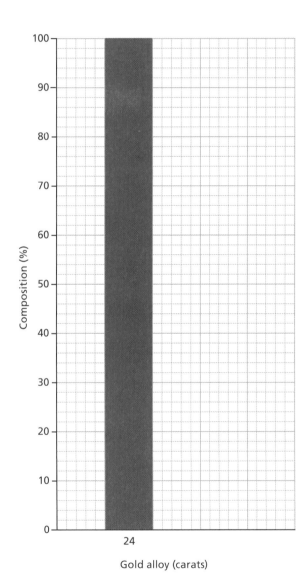

Magnesium reacts with dilute hydrochloric acid to form hydrogen gas.

A student is investigating how the mass changes during the reaction. The student uses the equipment shown in the figure. The table shows the student's results.

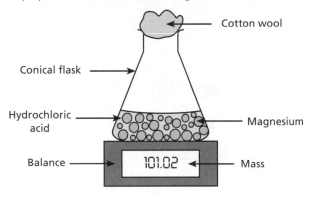

Time (s)	Mass (g)
0	200
20	188
40	176
60	168
80	161
100	155
120	151

Plot the data from the table on the graph below. **[2 marks]**

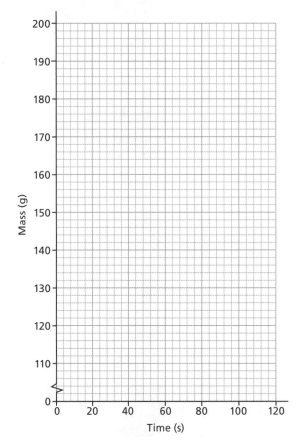

A student investigated the rate of reaction between marble chips and hydrochloric acid (HCl).

The table shows the results.

Time (s)	Volume of gas (dm³)
0	0.000
30	0.030
60	0.046
90	0.052
120	0.065
150	0.070
180	0.076

Plot the data from the table on the graph below.   **[3 marks]**

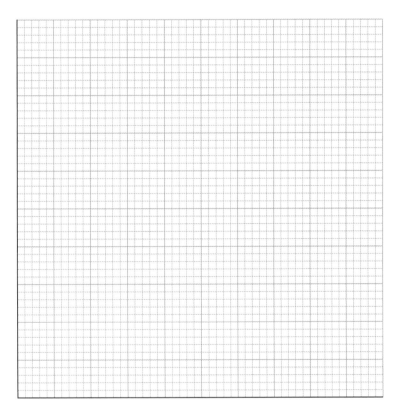

Time (s)

Total score: .... **/ 6**

Compare

Describe the similarities and/or differences between two things, rather than writing about one.

Example question

1 **The Rate and Extent of Chemical Change** P2 • Grade 1–3 🔢

A student investigated the rate of reaction between magnesium metal and hydrochloric acid.

The student completed the experiment with magnesium ribbon.

The sketch graph shows the results.

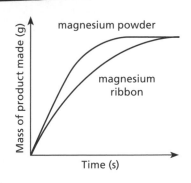

Compare the line of best fit for magnesium ribbon with magnesium powder. Tick (✔) **one** box.   **[1 mark]**

The line of best fit for a higher surface area would have a less steep slope.

⬜

The line of best fit for a higher surface area would have slopes with the same steepness.

⬜

The line of best fit for a higher surface area would have a steeper slope.

⬜

Complete the example

2   Bonding, Structure, and the Properties of Matter ⓟ • Grade 1–3

Covalent bonds hold the atoms together in a water molecule. There are intermolecular forces of attraction between different water molecules.

The figure shows a diagram of water molecules interacting.

Compare the strength of covalent bonds to intermolecular forces.

Tick (✓) **one** box.   **[1 mark]**

> Think about how much energy would be needed to separate the oxygen and hydrogen atoms in a molecule of water. Compare this to how much energy would be needed to overcome the intermolecular forces when melting ice (solid water) into liquid water.

Covalent bonds are weaker than intermolecular forces.   ☐

Covalent bonds are the same strength as intermolecular forces.   ☐

Covalent bonds are stronger than intermolecular forces.   ☐

3   Organic Chemistry ⓟ • Grade 4–5

Ethene is an alkene and ethane is an alkane. The figure shows the displayed structural formulae of ethene and of ethane.

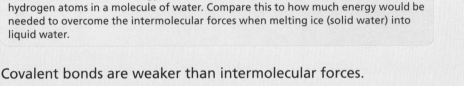

Ethene   Ethane

Compare the structure and bonding of ethane with ethene.   **[4 marks]**

Both ethene and ethane are _____, which are made of only

carbon and hydrogen held together by _____ bonds. Both ethene

and ethane are small _____.

Although both ethene and ethane have _____ carbon atoms in

each molecule, _____ contains a C=C double bond, whereas

_____ only has single bonds.

Exam practice questions

1   Bonding, Structure, and the Properties of Matter Ⓟ • Grade 1–3 🔢

Metallic elements make coarse particles that are cubes and fine particles that are cubes. The length of a coarse particle is 10 times larger than the length of a fine particle cube.

Compare the surface area to volume ratio of a coarse particle cube compared to a fine particle cube.

Tick (✓) **one** box.   **[1 mark]**

The surface area to volume ratio of a coarse particle is 10 times greater than that of a fine particle. ☐

The surface area to volume ratio of a coarse particle is the same as that of a fine particle. ☐

The surface area to volume ratio of a coarse particle is 10 times smaller than that of a fine particle. ☐

2   Bonding, Structure, and the Properties of Matter Ⓟ • Grade 4–5

The table shows the structure of three different forms of carbon.

Substance	Graphite	Diamond	Buckminsterfullerene
Structure			

Compare the structure and bonding of the different forms of carbon.   **[4 marks]**

....

....

....

....

....

....

3 Atomic Structure and the Periodic Table ⓟ₁ • Grade 6–7

Metals are found towards the left and centre of the Periodic Table.

Some of the properties of two transition metals and two Group 1 metals are shown in the table.

	Transition elements		Group 1 elements	
	Copper	Manganese	Lithium	Potassium
Melting point (°C)	1085	1246	181	64
Formula of oxides	CuO Cu_2O	MnO Mn_3O_4 Mn_2O_3 MnO_2 MnO_3 Mn_2O_7	Li_2O	K_2O

Compare the chemical and physical properties of transition metals and Group 1 metals.

Use the data in the table and your own knowledge.   **[6 marks]**

....

....

....

....

....

....

....

....

4 Using Resources ⓟ₂ • Grade 6–7

Polymers can be grouped into two types: thermosoftening and thermosetting.

The figure shows a diagram of the structures of each type of polymer.

Thermosoftening   Thermosetting

Compare the structure and bonding of thermosetting and thermosoftening polymers. **[4 marks]**

....

....

....

....

....

Total score: .... **/ 15**

Estimate

Find an approximate value.

Worked example and more!

TOP TIP
It may be a calculation where the result is not exact but based on sampling, or it could involve a graph where you need to find an approximate value.

Example question

1 **Atomic Structure and the Periodic Table P1 • Grade 1–3**

Group 1 metals are all solids at room temperature.

The table shows the melting point of the Group 1 metals.

Element	Lithium	Sodium	Potassium	Rubidium
Melting point (°C)	180	98	63	39

Estimate the melting point of francium. **[1 mark]**

Complete the example

2   Atomic Structure and the Periodic Table P1 • Grade 6–7 🖩

Element X has two stable isotopes. Their mass numbers are 63 and 65.

The percentage abundance of each isotope is:

- 70% of $_{29}^{63}X$

- 30% of $_{29}^{65}X$

Estimate the relative atomic mass of X.

Tick (✓) **one** box.   **[1 mark]**

> This question is not asking you to complete a full calculation. You are being asked to look at the numbers and make a judgement call. The relative atomic mass is a weighted average considering the mass and abundance of the isotopes. There is more of the lighter isotope than the heavier isotope. Therefore, the weighted average will be closer to the lighter isotope than the heavier isotope.

Less than 63   ☐

Between 63 and 64   ☐

Between 64 and 65   ☐

Greater than 65   ☐

Exam practice questions

1   Organic Chemistry P2 • Grade 1–3 🖩

Alkanes are hydrocarbons found in crude oil.

The table shows some information about alkanes.

Alkane	Molecular formula	Boiling point (°C)
Methane	CH_4	−162
Ethane	C_2H_6	−89
Propane	C_3H_8	−42

Estimate the boiling point of butane.   **[1 mark]**

The bar chart shows the densities of some alkali metals.

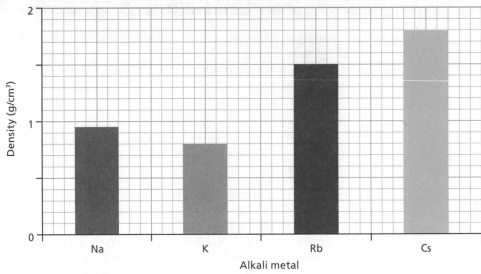

Estimate the density of lithium.   **[1 mark]**

....

Halogens are non-metal elements.

The table shows the boiling point of the Group 7 halogens.

Element	Boiling point (°C)
Fluorine	−188
Bromine	60
Iodine	184
Astatine	337

Estimate the boiling point of chlorine.   **[1 mark]**

....

4 Using Resources P2 • Grade 4–5 🖩

Alloys are chemical formulations which are often more useful than a pure metal.

Steel is an alloy mainly made of iron with other elements added.

The pie chart shows the composition of stainless steel.

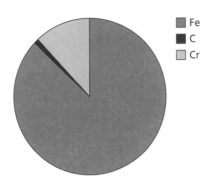

- Fe
- C
- Cr

a) Estimate the percentage of iron in stainless steel.   [1 mark]

....

b) Estimate the fraction of chromium in stainless steel.   [1 mark]

....

5 Chemistry of the Atmosphere P2 • Grade 6–7 🖩

The percentage of water vapour in the atmosphere can vary.

4.2 dm³ of air contains 0.05 dm³ of water vapour.

Estimate the percentage of water vapour in the air. Give your answer to 1 significant figure.   [2 marks]

....

Total score: .... / 7

Predict

Give a plausible outcome or result.

Worked example and more!

TOP TIP
A prediction doesn't have to be what will actually happen but it should show your scientific knowledge and understanding.

Example question

1

Atomic Structure and the Periodic Table P1 • Grade 1–3

Iron is a transition metal. Iron can react with halogens to make iron(III) halides. The table shows the results of these reactions.

Halogen	Observation
Fluorine	Violent reaction with bright flame
Chlorine	A fast reaction with an orange flame
Bromine	A quick reaction with an orange glow

a)   Predict what you would observe when iodine reacts with iron.   **[1 mark]**

b)   Predict the product of the reaction between chlorine and iron.   **[1 mark]**

Complete the example

2 Atomic Structure and the Periodic Table ⓟ1 • Grade 4–5

Halogens are Group 7 elements. The table gives information about the physical appearance of the halogens at room temperature.

Halogen	Physical appearance at room temperature
Fluorine	Pale yellow gas
Chlorine	Pale green gas
Bromine	Brown liquid
Iodine	Grey solid
Astatine	

Predict the physical appearance of astatine.   [2 marks]

....

There is 1 mark for the colour and 1 mark for the correct state at room temperature.

3 The Rate and Extent of Chemical Change ⓟ2 • Grade 8–9

In industry, sulfuric acid is produced using the Contact Process. The diagram shows the Contact Process.

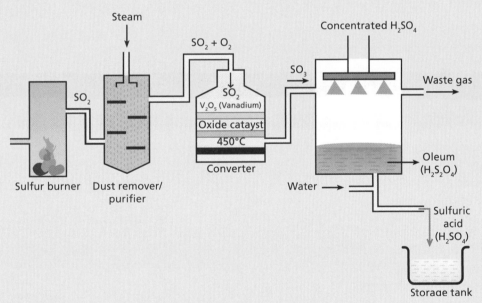

A reversible reaction happens in the converter. The balanced symbol equation for this reaction is: $2SO_2(g) + O_2(g) \rightleftharpoons 2SO_3(g)$

The forward reaction is exothermic.

Predict the effect of increasing temperature on the position of equilibrium.   [2 marks]

.... *sulfur dioxide will be made. The*

reaction will be favoured.

Exam practice questions

1   Chemical Changes ⓟ • Grade 1–3 😊

A student investigated the electrolysis of copper(II) sulfate solution. The figure shows a diagram of the equipment used.

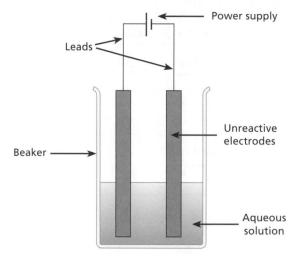

Bubbles of gas were collected at the positive electrode.

a)   Predict the observation at the negative electrode.   **[1 mark]**

....

b)   Predict how the colour of the solution would change during electrolysis.   **[2 marks]**

....

2   The Rate and Extent of Chemical Change ⓟ • Grade 4–5 😊

A student investigated the rate of reaction between magnesium ribbon and hydrochloric acid. The equipment used and a graph of the results are shown below.

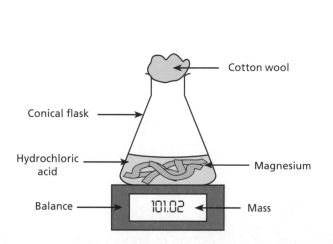

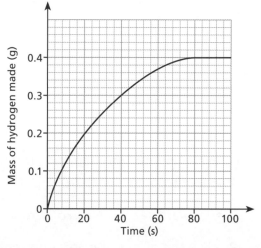

The reaction was monitored for 100 seconds and there was magnesium left behind.

a) Predict the effect on the rate of reaction if a higher concentration of hydrochloric acid was used. [1 mark]

b) Predict the effect on the maximum mass of hydrogen produced if magnesium powder was used instead of magnesium ribbon. [1 mark]

c) Predict the effect of increasing the temperature. [1 mark]

3 The Rate and Extent of Chemical Change P2 / Energy Changes P1 / Using Resources P2 • Grade 6–7

The Haber process is used in industry to manufacture ammonia.

The figure shows a diagram of the process.

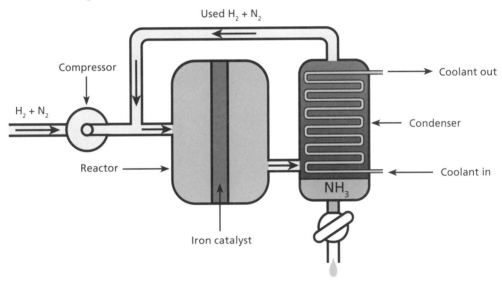

The balanced symbol equation for this reaction is:

$$N_2(g) + 3H_2(g) \rightleftharpoons 2NH_3(g)$$

a) Predict the effect of increasing the pressure on the position of equilibrium. [2 marks]

b) Predict the effect of removing the iron-based catalyst on the Haber process. [4 marks]

Total score: _____ / 12

Evaluate

Use the information supplied, as well as your knowledge and understanding, to consider evidence for and against when making a judgement / claim.

Worked example and more!

TOP TIP
Consider:
What is the judgement?
How is it supported and opposed by evidence?
How well is the evidence connected to the judgement?

Example question

1 Chemical Changes **P1** • Grade 4–5

Zinc (Zn) is a metal. It is extracted from zinc oxide (ZnO). All other solid products from the extraction method must be separated from the zinc.

The table shows information about three possible methods to extract zinc from zinc oxide.

Method	Reactant	Relative cost	Products
1	Hydrogen gas	High	Zinc solid Water gas
2	Coke	Low	Zinc solid Carbon dioxide gas
3	Iron	Low	Zinc solid Iron oxide solid

Evaluate the three possible methods for extracting zinc from zinc oxide. **[4 marks]**

Complete the example

The table shows the properties of some materials that could be used to make a kayak frame.

Material	Relative strength	Relative stiffness	Density (g/cm³)
Wood	0.1	10	0.71
Polymer	30	50	0.3
Carbon nanotube	60	1000	1.3

Evaluate the use of the materials to make a kayak. **[4 marks]**

.... is the least dense of the materials and it will make the
.... kayak.

However, polymer and wood kayaks are more likely to ....

Therefore, the .... is the best material as it is the stiffest
material and very strong, therefore durable.

However, a kayak made from carbon nanotube would need to have
.... space compared to the other materials because carbon
nanotube is .... than water.

Exam practice questions

The table shows information about two different ways to power electric cars.

	Hydrogen fuel cell	Rechargeable lithium-ion battery
Refuel or recharge time (arbitrary units)	5	30
Maximum distance on one fuel or charge (arbitrary units)	400	250
Comparison of distance travelled for same energy (arbitrary units)	1	3
Comparison of cost for fuel or refuelling (arbitrary units)	16	1
Comparison of purchase price of the vehicle (arbitrary units)	10	3

Evaluate the use of hydrogen fuel cells compared with rechargeable lithium-ion batteries to power electric cars. Use the table and your own knowledge.   **[6 marks]**

....

....

....

....

....

....

....

....

2 Using Resources ℗2 • Grade 4–5

The table shows information about two different materials used to make drinks bottles.

	Glass	Plastic
Raw material	Sand, limestone, salt	Crude oil
Bottle material	Soda-lime glass	Polypropene
Maximum temperature used in production	1600°C	850°C
Number of times reused	25	0
Percentage of recycled material used in new bottles	50	10
Fossil fuel use to produce and transport (arbitrary units)	4320	2639

Evaluate the sustainability of the production of drinks bottles made from soda-lime glass and polypropene.

Use the table and your own knowledge.   **[6 marks]**

....

....

....

....

....

....

....

....

....

3 Organic Chemistry ⓟ2 • Grade 6–7

Polymers can be used to make uniforms for firefighters.

The table shows information about two different materials that can be used to make uniforms for firefighters.

	Poly(propene)	Polyester
Melting point (°C)	165	260
Flame resistance	Low	High
Water absorbance	Low	High
Mass per 1 cm³ (g)	0.9	1.4

Evaluate the use of these two materials for making uniforms for firefighters. **[4 marks]**

....

....

....

....

....

4 Using Resources ⓟ2 • Grade 6–7

Food plates can be made from ceramics, polymers or paper. The table shows information about plates with the same diameter.

	Ceramic	Polymer	Paper
Raw material	Mined clay	Crude oil	Wood
Maximum packed in delivery box	50	100	500
Average use	1000	400	1
Recycle	No	Yes	Yes
Biodegradable	No	No	Yes

Evaluate the use of these materials for making food plates. You should use features of life cycle assessments (LCAs), the information in the table and your own knowledge. **[4 marks]**

....

....

....

....

....

Total score: .... / 20

Justify

Support a case or argument with evidence. This evidence is usually from data provided in the question.

Worked example and more!

> **TOP TIP**
> Unlike 'Evaluate' questions, you do not need to give arguments for and against.

Example question

1

Atomic Structure and the Periodic Table P1 • Grade 4–5

The model of the structure of the atom has changed over time.

In one experiment, positively charged alpha radiation was fired at a sheet of very thin gold foil. The diagram shows the experiment.

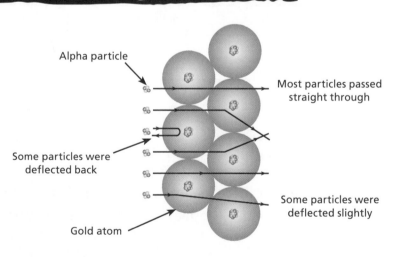

Alpha particle

Most particles passed straight through

Some particles were deflected back

Some particles were deflected slightly

Gold atom

The data from the experiment was used to conclude that:

- atoms were mainly empty space
- atoms had a small positive centre, where most of the mass is found.

Justify the conclusions. **[6 marks]**

Complete the example

Hydrogen is an element and a gas at room temperature.

The figure shows the position and symbol of hydrogen in the Periodic Table.

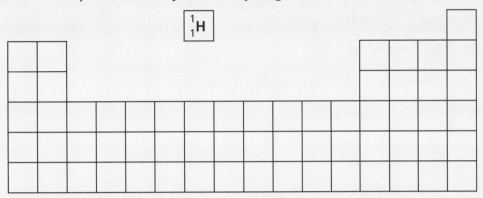

Hydrogen can form two stable ions by losing or gaining one electron.

When hydrogen is fully oxidised, it makes water and this has pH 7.

a) Justify that hydrogen belongs in Group 1 of the Periodic Table. [2 marks]

All Group 1 elements have _____ electron in their outer shell.

Hydrogen only has one _____ and therefore it is in the outer shell of the atom.

b) Justify that hydrogen belongs in Group 7 of the Periodic Table. [4 marks]

All Group 7 elements need _____ electron in their outer shell to gain _____ configuration.

Hydrogen only has one _____ and therefore has only the first outer shell occupied.

So, hydrogen also needs one electron to _____ its outer shell and have noble gas configuration.

c) Justify that hydrogen is neither a metal nor a non-metal. [3 marks]

Metal oxides are _____ and non-metal oxides are _____.

Hydrogen oxide, or water, is _____. Therefore, hydrogen is neither a metal nor a non-metal.

Exam practice questions

1 **Chemical Changes P1 • Grade 4–5 🔒**

A student investigated the reaction of magnesium with different types of acid.

This was the method used:

1. 10 cm³ of the same concentration of each acid or pure water was measured and put into separate, labelled test tubes.

2. 0.1 g of magnesium metal was added to each test tube.

3. The reaction was observed.

Here is a diagram of the results.

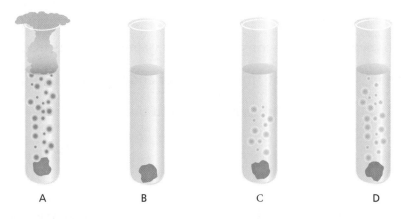

a) Justify that test tube B was the control and contained pure water.   **[4 marks]**

....

....

....

....

b) Write the four liquids in order of reactivity with the most reactive first.

   Justify your order of reactivity.   **[3 marks]**

....

....

....

....

....

2 Energy Changes ⓟ • Grade 8-9

A student investigated simple cells using the equipment shown in the diagram.

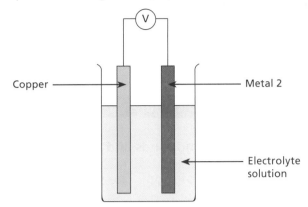

If Metal 2 is more reactive than copper, then the voltage measured is positive. If copper is more reactive than Metal 2, then the voltage measured is negative. The bigger the difference in reactivity of the two metals, the larger the voltage produced.

The student's results are shown in the table.

Metal 2	Voltage (V)
A	−0.8
B	1.2
C	0.8
D	−0.4

a) The student says that two electrodes of the same metal would not be useful.

Justify the student's statement. [1 mark]

_____

b) Metal A was the least reactive.

Justify this statement. [2 marks]

_____

3 Organic Chemistry ⓟ • Grade 8-9

Crude oil is a mixture of hydrocarbons.

Justify the need for cracking of hydrocarbons. [4 marks]

_____

_____

_____

_____

_____

_____

Total score: .... / 14

Mixed Questions

1 | Atomic Structure and the Periodic Table P1 • Grade 1–3

This question is about elements, compounds and mixtures.

a) Substance A has only one type of atom. The substance can conduct electricity.
What type of substance is A? Tick (✔) **one** box. **[1 mark]**

Metal alloy ☐   Pure metal element ☐   Impure non-metal compound ☐

b) Substance B is made of more than one type of particle. The particles are not in fixed proportions. The substance can conduct electricity.

What type of substance is B? Tick (✔) **one** box. **[1 mark]**

Metal alloy ☐   Pure metal element ☐   Pure non-metal element ☐

c) Substance C is an element found in group 7.
What is the name for the elements found in Group 7? Tick (✔) **one** box. **[1 mark]**

Alkali metals ☐   Transition metals ☐

Halogens ☐   Noble gases ☐

d) Substance D is an element found in Group 1.

Give the charge on the ion of substance D. **[1 mark]**

e) Substance E is a compound made from substance A and D.

The diagram shows the compound structure.

Determine the empirical formula of substance E. **[1 mark]**

+ A   D

2 | Using Resources P2 • Grade 1–3

Ammonia can be used to make fertilisers. Ammonia is made in the Haber process.

a) Complete the word equation for making ammonia from its elements. **[2 marks]**

.... + ... ⇌ ammonia

b) What temperature does the Haber process happen at? Tick (✔) **one** box.   **[1 mark]**

20°C ☐   100°C ☐   450°C ☐   750°C ☐

c) Describe how the ammonia gas is removed from the reactor.   **[2 marks]**

....

....

3 **Bonding, Structure, and the Properties of Matter ⓟ • Grade 4–5**

Carbon forms different structures at room temperature and pressure.

The diagrams show five different carbon structures.

- ⬤ carbon atom
- —— bond
- - - - - intermolecular force of attraction

a) Name the bonding found in all carbon structures.   **[1 mark]**

....

b) Describe the shape of Buckminsterfullerene.   **[1 mark]**

....

c) Give **one** use of graphene.   **[1 mark]**

....

d) Explain why graphite and graphene can conduct electricity.   **[3 marks]**

....

....

e) Explain why diamond has a high melting point but Buckminsterfullerene has a lower melting point.   **[6 marks]**

....

....

4 Chemistry of the Atmosphere ⓟ2 • Grade 4–5

This question is about the proportions of different gases in the atmosphere.

a) Give the approximate percentage of dry air made of nitrogen. **[1 mark]**

b) Write the formula of the gas which makes up about $\frac{1}{5}$ of dry air. **[1 mark]**

c) Name **two** greenhouse gases. **[2 marks]**

d) Explain the importance of greenhouse gases in the Earth's atmosphere. **[2 marks]**

5 Chemical Changes ⓟ1 • Grade 6–7 ▦ ☺

A student plans to complete a titration to find out the volume of nitric acid that reacts with 25 cm³ of 0.1 mol dm⁻³ solution of potassium hydroxide.

The diagram shows the equipment used.

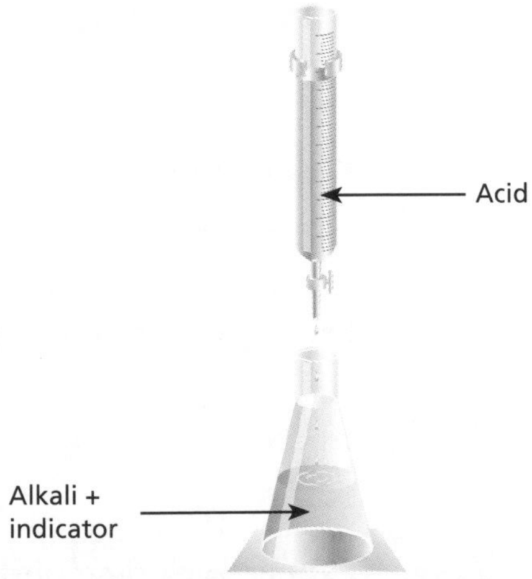

a) Plan the titration experiment to reliably measure the volume of nitric acid required to neutralise 25 cm³ of 0.1 mol dm⁻³ solution of potassium hydroxide.

You do not need to mention safety. **[6 marks]**

Acid

Alkali + indicator

....

....

....

b) Calculate the number of moles of potassium hydroxide used in this investigation. **[3 marks]**

....

....

....

c) Explain why nitric acid is classified as a strong acid. **[2 marks]**

....

....

....

d) Complete the ionic equation for the reaction between nitric acid and potassium hydroxide. **[2 marks]**

..............................(aq) + ...(aq) → H_2O (l)

6 | Using Resources $P2$ • Grade 8–9

Crude oil is a mixture of hydrocarbons.

a) Explain how crude oil is separated. **[4 marks]**

....

....

....

....

b) Complete the balanced symbol equation for the cracking of decane, $C_{10}H_{22}$. **[1 mark]**

$C_{10}H_{22}$ → 2.............................. + C_6H_{14}

c) Plan a method to show that decane is saturated but the products of cracking decane are unsaturated. **[3 marks]**

....

....

....

....

....

Total score: .... **/ 49**

Index of Topics

This grid tells you which questions in this book offer practice for each of the 10 specification topics.

Topic	Page	Question	Example Question	Complete the Example	Exam Practice Question
Atomic Structure and the Periodic Table, Paper 1	9	3		✓	
	10	2			✓
	10	3			✓
	12	1	✓		
	17	3		✓	
	17	1			✓
	18	5			✓
	20	1	✓		
	21	3		✓	
	22	3			✓
	24	1	✓		
	28	10			✓
	30	1	✓		
	34	2	✓		
	35	3		✓	
	37	3			✓
	40	2	✓		
	41	4		✓	
	43	3			✓
	46	2	✓		
	48	1			✓
	51	3		✓	
	52	2			✓
	58	1	✓		
	60	1			✓
	63	3		✓	
	67	3		✓	
	68	2			✓
	68	3			✓
	80	2	✓		
	81	1			✓
	82	1	✓		
	82	2	✓		
	99	3			✓
	100	1	✓		
	101	2		✓	
	102	2			✓
	102	3			✓
	103	5			✓
	104	1	✓		
	105	2		✓	
	112	1	✓		
	113	2		✓	
	116	1			✓

Topic	Page	Question	Example Question	Complete the Example	Exam Practice Question
Bonding, Structure, and the Properties of Matter, Paper 1	5	1			✓
	8	2	✓		
	19	6			✓
	26	3			✓
	27	6			✓
	29	11			✓
	36	2			✓
	38	6			✓
	39	8			✓
	39	9			✓
	41	3		✓	
	46	1	✓		
	52	2			✓
	53	3			✓
	64	3			✓
	66	1	✓		
	68	2			✓
	70	6			✓
	78	1			✓
	84	1			✓
	97	2		✓	
	98	1			✓
	98	2			✓
	109	2		✓	
	117	3			✓
Quantitative Chemistry, Paper 1	11	5			✓
	28	9			✓
	32	4			✓
	44	6			✓
	49	3			✓
	67	3		✓	
	71	7			✓
	71	8			✓
	72	2	✓		
	73	3		✓	
	73	4		✓	
	74	3			✓
	74	4			✓
	79	3			✓
	79	4			✓
	83	3		✓	
	83	4		✓	

Topic	Page	Question	Example Question	Complete the Example	Exam Practice Question
Quantitative Chemistry, Paper 1	85	3			✓
	85	4			✓
	89	4			✓
Chemical Changes, Paper 1	4	1	✓		
	7	4			✓
	12	1	✓		
	14	3			✓
	15	4			✓
	15	5			✓
	16	2	✓		
	22	4			✓
	25	3		✓	
	28	8			✓
	31	4		✓	
	32	4			✓
	33	5			✓
	33	6			✓
	34	1	✓		
	35	4		✓	
	35	5		✓	
	37	4			✓
	39	9			✓
	44	5			✓
	44	6			✓
	59	4		✓	
	61	3			✓
	62	2	✓		
	65	4			✓
	67	1			✓
	69	5			✓
	71	8			✓
	72	2	✓		
	74	3			✓
	74	4			✓
	79	4			✓
	81	4		✓	
	81	3			✓
	87	3		✓	
	88	2			✓
	89	3			✓
	92	3		✓	
	106	1			✓
	108	1	✓		
	114	1			✓
	118	5			✓
Energy Changes, Paper 1	4	2	✓		
	6	3			✓
	8	1	✓		
	23	5			✓
	26	5			✓
	32	2			✓
	42	2			✓
	55	2		✓	
	57	3			✓

Topic	Page	Question	Example Question	Complete the Example	Exam Practice Question
Energy Changes, Paper 1	57	4			✓
	58	2	✓		
	60	2			✓
	63	4		✓	
	78	2			✓
	107	3			✓
	109	1			✓
	115	2			✓
The Rate and Extent of Chemical Change, Paper 2	13	3		✓	
	14	2			✓
	27	7			✓
	45	7			✓
	54	1	✓		
	55	2		✓	
	56	2			✓
	64	2			✓
	67	3		✓	
	69	4			✓
	72	1	✓		
	74	2			✓
	77	3		✓	
	84	2			✓
	87	4		✓	
	91	2		✓	
	94	2			✓
	95	3			✓
	96	1	✓		
	105	3		✓	
	106	2			✓
	107	3			✓
Organic Chemistry, Paper 2	5	3		✓	
	9	1			✓
	13	1			✓
	15	6			✓
	18	3			✓
	19	7			✓
	20	2	✓		
	21	1			✓
	21	2			✓
	24	2	✓		
	26	4			✓
	29	11			✓
	30	2	✓		
	38	5			✓
	43	4			✓
	44	6			✓
	50	2	✓		
	51	4		✓	
	53	4			✓
	57	3			✓
	65	5			✓
	75	6			✓
	76	1	✓		
	77	4		✓	

Topic	Page	Question	Example Question	Complete the Example	Exam Practice Question
Organic Chemistry, Paper 2	80	1	✓		
	81	2			✓
	97	3		✓	
	101	1			✓
	111	3			✓
	115	3			✓
Chemical Analysis, Paper 2	6	2			✓
	10	4			✓
	17	2			✓
	21	4		✓	
	25	4		✓	
	25	2			✓
	31	3		✓	
	35	4		✓	
	36	1			✓
	37	4			✓
	40	2	✓		
	45	8			✓
	52	1			✓
	67	2		✓	
	75	5			✓
	76	2	✓		
	86	2	✓		
	88	1			✓
Chemistry of the Atmosphere, Paper 2	7	5			✓
	9	1			✓
	16	1	✓		
	18	3			✓
	18	4			✓
	25	1			✓
	32	1			✓
	32	3			✓
	40	1	✓		
	47	3		✓	

Topic	Page	Question	Example Question	Complete the Example	Exam Practice Question
Chemistry of the Atmosphere, Paper 2	50	1	✓		
	61	4			✓
	73	1			✓
	79	3			✓
	90	1	✓		
	103	5			✓
	118	4			✓
Using Resources, Paper 2	29	12			✓
	38	7			✓
	41	3		✓	
	42	1			✓
	42	4			✓
	48	2			✓
	55	3		✓	
	56	1			✓
	59	3		✓	
	62	1	✓		
	64	1			✓
	65	5			✓
	71	7			✓
	72	1	✓		
	81	3		✓	
	85	3			✓
	86	1	✓		
	89	4			✓
	93	1			✓
	99	4			✓
	103	4			✓
	107	3			✓
	109	2		✓	
	110	2			✓
	111	4			✓
	116	2			✓
	119	6			✓

Answers

Pages 4–7: Choose

Complete the example

3. **Carboxylic acid** is a weak acid. When an **alcohol** reacts with **carboxylic acid**, a sweet smelling **ester** is made.

Exam practice questions

1.   A = Solid   [1]
      B = Liquid   [1]
      C = Gas   [1]
2.   chlorine   [1]
      hydrogen   [1]
3.   **a)** increased   [1]
      b) an exothermic   [1]
4.   increase   [1]
      limiting   [1]
      excess   [1]
      evaporating   [1]
5.   A = carbon dioxide (*Accept* water)   [1]
      B = oxygen   [1]
      C = nitrogen   [1]

Pages 8–11: Give

Complete the example

3.   **a)** *Any two from:* (sodium) floats; (sodium) melts / forms a ball / forms a sphere; (sodium) moves around; sodium becomes smaller (*Allow* sodium disappears); effervescence (*Allow* fizzing *or* bubbles)
      b) H_2

Exam practice questions

1.   **a)** Oxygen   [1]
      b) Carbon dioxide   [1]
      c) Acid rain   [1]
2.   Protons 11; Electrons 11   [1]
      Neutrons 13   [1]
3.   **a)** Halogens   [1]
      b) Cl_2 [1]
      c) Na^+ (*Accept* Na^{1+} *or* Na^{+1})   [1]
           Cl^- (*Accept* Cl^{1-} *or* Cl^{-1})   [1]
4.   Step 1: Pencil is insoluble in water / It prevents the start line from running into the results.   [1]
      Step 3: To ensure the solvent wicks through the paper / To prevent samples from dissolving into the solvent / To ensure that separation happens.   [1]
5.   **a)** 6.02×10^{23} [1]
      b) 0.00024 = 0.24 g   [1]
           Moles = $\frac{0.24}{63.5}$ = 0.00378   [1]
           Number of atoms = $0.00378 \times 6.02 \times 10^{23}$ [1]
           Number of atoms = 2.27556×10^{21} [1]
           = 2.27×10^{21} [1]

Pages 12–15: Identify

Complete the example

3.   **a)** Concentration of hydrochloric acid
      b) Time (taken for cross to disappear)

Exam practice questions

1.   **a)** *One from:* –OH; hydroxy (*Accept a circle around the functional group in the diagram*)   [1]
      b) A (*Accept* methanol)   [1]
           D (*Accept* ethanol)   [1]
      c) *Accept one from:* carboxylic acid; ethanoic acid; B   [1]
2.   **a)** Volume of gas   [1]
      b) *Accept one from:* concentration of hydrogen peroxide; volume of hydrogen peroxide; temperature of reaction mixture   [1]
3.   **a)** Oxygen / O_2 [1]
      b) Oxidation   [1]
4.   **a)** Stage 1: (thermal) decomposition   [1]
           Stage 2: REDOX   [1]
      b) Carbon (*Accept* graphite)   [1]
5.   **a)** Fe_2O_3 (*Accept* iron oxide *or* iron ore)   [1]
      b) CO_2 / carbon dioxide   [1]
6.   **a)** –COOH   [1]
      b) Irritation of the skin / eye (from the acidic liquid / nettles).   [1]

Pages 16–19: Name

Complete the example

3.   **a)** Sodium **chloride**
      b) Lithium and **bromine**

Exam practice questions

1.   **a)** Proton   [1]
      b) Neutron   [1]
      c) (Niels) Bohr   [1]
2.   **a)** Sodium hydroxide / NaOH   [1]
      b) Barium chloride / $BaCl_2$ [1]
3.   **a)** Methane / CH_4 [1]
      b) Combustion   [1]
      c) Carbon dioxide / CO_2 [1]
4.   *In any order:* Carbon dioxide; Methane   [2]
5.   X = Electron   [1]
6.   **a)** Metallic bonding   [1]
      b) Electrons   [1]
      c) Ionic bonding   [1]
      d) Ions   [1]
7.   **a)** Fractional distillation and cracking   [1]
      b) Carbon dioxide and water   [1]
      c) Ethanol   [1]

Pages 20–23: Write

Complete the example

3.   chlorine + **potassium bromide** ➔ **potassium chloride + bromine**
     (*Accept reactants in either order*)
4. Ag^+ **+ I^- ➔ AgI**

Exam practice questions

1.   octane + oxygen ➔ carbon dioxide + water
     (*Accept reactants in either order; accept products in either order*)   [2]

2. ethanol + oxygen → carbon dioxide + water
(Accept reactants in either order; accept products in either order) **[2]**

3. $2K + 2H_2O \rightarrow 2KOH + H_2$
(1 mark for correct reactants in either order; 1 mark for correct products in either order; 1 mark for correct balancing) **[3]**

4. a) $2Cl^- \rightarrow Cl_2 + 2e^-$
(1 mark for correct reactant formula; 1 mark for correct product formulae in either order; 1 mark for correct balancing) **[3]**

b) $Cu^{2+} + 2e^- \rightarrow Cu$
(1 mark for correct reactant formulae in either order; 1 mark for correct product formula; 1 mark for correct balancing) **[3]**

5. a) $2H_2 \rightarrow 4H^+ + 4e^-$
(1 mark for correct reactant formula; 1 mark for correct product formulae in either order; 1 mark for correct balancing) **[3]**

b) $O_2 + 4H^+ + 4e^- \rightarrow 2H_2O$
(1 mark for correct reactant formulae in any order; 1 mark for correct product formula; 1 mark for correct balancing) **[3]**

Pages 24–29: Complete
Complete the example
3. magnesium + **oxygen** → **magnesium oxide**

4. Chromatography can be used to separate mixtures and can give information to **(help) identify** substances.

Exam practice questions
1. **carbon dioxide** + water → glucose + **oxygen** **[2]**

2. CO_2 **(g)** + $Ca(OH)_2$ **(aq)** → $CaCO_3$ **(s)** + H_2O **(l)** **[4]**

3.

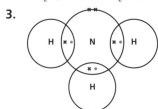

(1 mark for each correct covalent bond; 1 mark for lone pair of electrons on the nitrogen) **[3]**

4. a) energy **[1]**
b) oxygen **[1]**
c) incomplete combustion **[1]**

5. surroundings **[1]**
decrease / get lower / fall **[1]**
exothermic reactions / exothermic changes / exothermic chemical reactions / exothermic chemical changes. **[1]**

6.

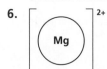

(1 mark for correct charge on magnesium ion; 1 mark for no electrons in the outer shell of magnesium ion; 1 mark for correct charge on oxide ion; 1 mark for eight electrons in the outer shell of oxide ion)

7. a) magnesium + hydrochloric acid → **magnesium chloride** + **hydrogen**
(1 mark for each in either order) **[2]**

b) The independent variable is **concentration (of hydrochloric acid)**. **[1]**
The dependent variable is **mass**. **[1]**

8. a) oxidised **[1]**
b) reduced **[1]**
c) free to move / free moving *(Accept liquid or aqueous solution)* **[1]**

9. a) moles *(Accept mol)* **[1]**
b) Avogadro constant *(Accept 6.02×10^{23})* **[1]**

10. a) salt *(Accept ionic compound)* **[1]**
b) Cl_2 **[1]** and Br_2 **[1]** *(Must be in this order.)*

11.

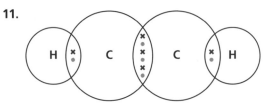

(1 mark for correct dots and crosses between each carbon and hydrogen atom; 1 mark for six electrons between the two carbon atoms) **[2]**

12. a) *Left-hand label:* Compressor **[1]**
Right-hand label: Condenser **[1]**

b) $3H_2\,(g) + N_2\,(g) \rightleftharpoons 2NH_3\,(g)$ **[3]**

Pages 30–33: Define
Complete the example
3. a) A single **element** / **compound**.
(You could also say 'not mixed with any other substance')

b) A substance that has had **nothing added to it**.
(You could also just say 'unadulterated')

4. a) Gain of **oxygen** and loss of **electrons**.
b) Loss of **oxygen** and gain of **electrons**.

Exam practice questions
1. Total amount of greenhouse gases / carbon dioxide emitted **[1]**
over the full life cycle of a product, service or event. **[1]**

2. a) Transfers energy to the surroundings **[1]**
so the temperature of the surroundings increases. **[1]**

b) The minimum amount of energy that particles must have to react. **[1]**

3. Water that is safe to drink. **[1]**

4. The reactant that is completely used up. **[1]**

5. An ionic compound **[1]**
that is melted or dissolved in water, **[1]**
which is able to conduct electricity. **[1]**

6. a) Close to the true value. **[1]**

b) The student repeats the investigation using the same method and equipment and obtains the same results. **[1]**

c) Repeated by another person, or by using different equipment or techniques, and the same results are obtained. **[1]**

Pages 34–39: Describe
Complete the example
3. **Filter** the mixture.
   Collect the **sand / solid / residue** in the **filter paper**.
   Dry the residue by **patting dry with absorbent paper / putting in a drying oven / drying with a hairdryer**.
4. a) The student would **see bubbles / hear fizzing / observe effervescence** and the zinc would **get smaller / disappear**.
   b) Use a **burning** splint.
      If the gas is hydrogen, you will hear a **(squeaky) pop**.
5. Take a small sample of the acid and add **universal indicator solution** to it or put a drop of the unknown acid on **universal indicator paper**.
   Compare the colour of the **universal indicator** to the colour chart to determine the **pH**. If the **pH** is less than 3 then the acid is **hydrochloric** acid. If the **pH** is greater than 4 but less than 7 then the acid is **methanoic** acid.

Exam practice questions
1. The food colouring is a mixture / formulation. **[1]**
   It is made of three different colours. **[1]**
2. *Any four from:* sodium (atom) loses an electron; chlorine (atom) gains an electron; chloride ion formed; chloride has negative charge / is a negative ion / particle; sodium ion formed; sodium has positive charge; oppositely charged ions attract; a giant structure / lattice is formed. **[4]**
3. a) In order of their atomic masses. **[1]**
   b) Mendeleev left gaps for elements that he thought had not been discovered. **[1]**
      Mendeleev changed the order based on atomic masses / ordered the elements by their chemical reactions. **[1]**
   c) No gaps **[1]**
      Group 0 / Noble gases discovered. **[1]**
      Elements listed by increasing atomic number. **[1]**
4. Chlorine: damp litmus paper **[1]**
          bleached / turns white **[1]**
   Hydrogen: a burning splint **[1]**
          pop sound **[1]**
   Oxygen: glowing splint **[1]**
          relights **[1]**
5. a) *Any catalyst from:* zeolite; aluminosilicate; silicon dioxide; silica; aluminium oxide; broken porcelain **[1]**
      Temperature of about 500°C (*Accept range from 500 ➔ 600°C*) **[1]**
   b) High temperature / over 800°C **[1]**
      Steam **[1]**
6. Silica forms a giant covalent structure **[1]**
   where the atoms are held together by shared **[1]**
   pairs of electrons **[1]**
   in strong covalent bonds. **[1]**
7. Use bacteria **[1]**
   to produce leachate solutions / solution which contain copper compounds. **[1]**
   Electrolysis of solution (containing a copper compound) **[1]**
   or displacement (of copper) from solution (containing a copper compound). **[1]**
8. *Any three from:*
   Need to know the effects of nanoparticles in the blood at this concentration.
   Need to find out the long-term risk of using sunscreen.
   The study needs to be repeated by other scientists.
   Need to check if the study was biased, e.g. carried out by a sunscreen manufacturer.
   Need to repeat using more volunteers.
   Need to repeat using a wider range of volunteers of different ages / sexes / skin types. **[3]**
9. REDOX is reduction and oxidation happening at the same time. **[1]**
   Aluminium atoms are oxidised. **[1]**
   Aluminium atoms lose electrons. **[1]**
   Chlorine atoms are reduced. **[1]**
   Chlorine atoms gain electrons. **[1]**

Pages 40–45: Why / What / Which / Where / When / Who / How
Complete the example
3. a) Mixture
      Formulation
   b) In pure metals, the layers of **atoms / ions** easily **slide** over each other, but in alloys, the different sizes of **atoms / ions** distort the layers so they can't **slide** as easily.
4. Each isotope has a different number of **neutrons.**

Exam practice questions
1. a) Water that is safe to drink **[1]**
   b) Chlorine **[1]**
   c) *Any two from:* To kill microorganisms; To prevent waterborne disease; To stop people from getting sick or ill. **[2]**
2. a) Independent **[1]**
   b) Control **[1]**
   c) Dependent **[1]**
3. a) Chadwick **[1]**
   b) In the nucleus of most atoms **[1]**
4. a) Propene **[1]**
   b) Addition polymerisation **[1]**
   c) Collect the used plastic bottles. **[1]**
      Wash them. **[1]**
      Melt them. **[1]**
      Re-shape them into new bottles. **[1]**
5. a) Copper(II) oxide and copper(II) carbonate only **[1]**
   b) By using an electric heater **[1]**
6. a) HCOOH (*Accept* CH_2O_2) **[1]**
   b) Has a –COOH functional group **[1]**
      Is an aqueous solution **[1]**
   c) 0.02 mol **[1]**
7. a) Top pan balance **[1]**
   b) No further mass change **[1]**

8. a) Separation depends on the distribution of substances between the phases. [1]
The greater the attraction of the dye to the paper, the shorter the distance the dye will travel. [1]
The more soluble the dye, the greater the distance travelled. [1]
b) Allow the solvent front to travel further. [1]
Use a different solvent. [1]

Pages 46–49: Use

Complete the example

3. a) *Any one from*: Nitrogen; N_2
b) *Any one from:* Noble gases; Group 0
c) $\frac{1}{5}$

Exam practice questions

1. a) *Any one from:* Fluorine; Chlorine
(*Accept* F, F_2, Cl, Cl_2) [1]
b) As you go down the group, melting point increases. (*Accept:* as you go up the group, melting point decreases.) [1]
c) Iodine [1]
2. a) 20 : 2 [1]
= 10 : 1 [1]
b) There are 55 atoms. [1]
There are 47 copper atoms. [1]
$\frac{47}{55} \times 100 = 85.454\,545\,45$ [1]
85.5% [1]
3. a) Only one spot on the chromatogram. [1]
b) $\frac{6}{12}$ [1]
= 0.5 [1]

Pages 50–53: Draw

Complete the example

3.

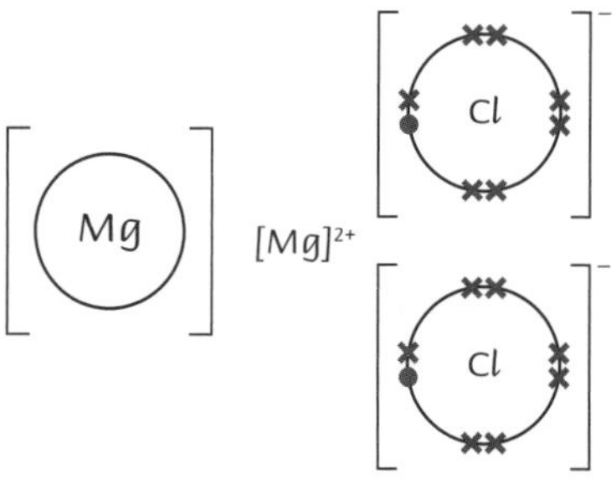
Mg
[Mg]2+
Cl
Cl

4.

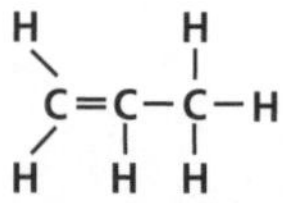

Exam practice questions

1. Hydrogen – Burning splint and hear a pop sound
Carbon dioxide – Limewater turns milky
Oxygen – Glowing splint relights
Chlorine – Damp litmus paper turns white
(All correct with no additional lines drawn; 2 marks for two or three correct; 1 mark for one correct) [3]

2. a)

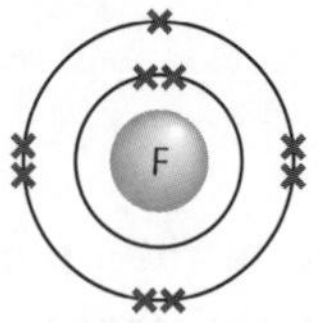
F

(1 mark for 9 electrons in total; 1 mark for two electrons in the first shell and seven electrons in the outer shell) [2]

b)

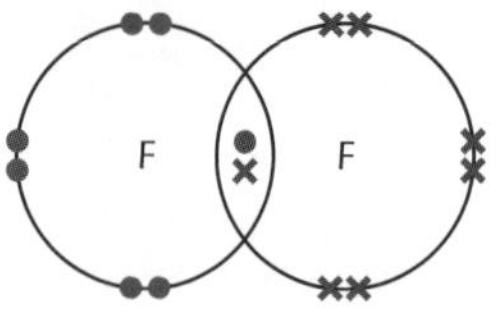
F
F

(1 mark for a shared pair of electrons between the atoms; 1 mark for each atom having 7 electrons in their outer shell) [2]

3. a)

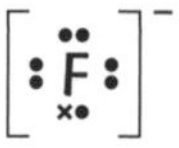

(1 mark for eight electrons in the outer shell; 1 mark for charge) [2]

b)

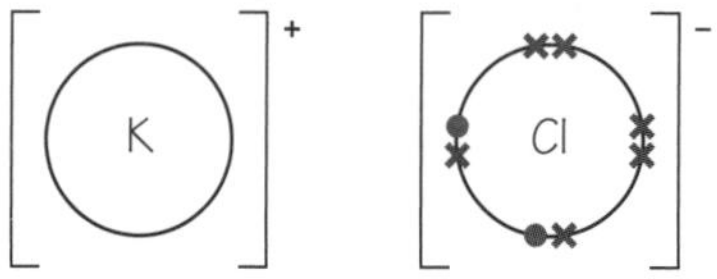
K
Cl

(1 mark for no electrons in potassium outer shell; 1 mark for charge on potassium ion; 1 mark for 8 electrons in the chloride outer shell; 1 mark for charge on chloride ion) [4]

4.

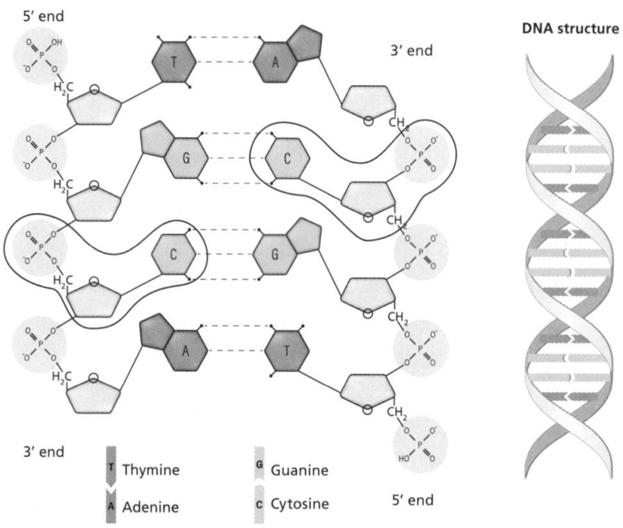
5′ end
3′ end
DNA structure
3′ end
5′ end
Thymine
Adenine
Guanine
Cytosine

(1 mark for each correct circle) [2]

Pages 54–57: Sketch

Complete the example

2.

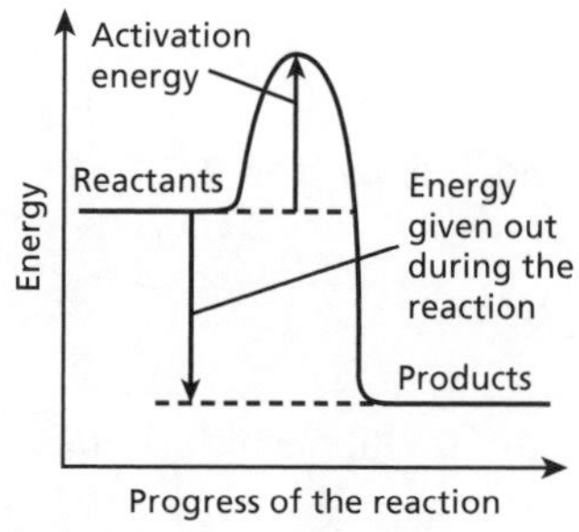
Activation energy
Reactants
Energy given out during the reaction
Products
Energy
Progress of the reaction

3. LD poly(ethene)

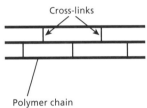

HD polyethene

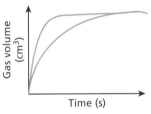

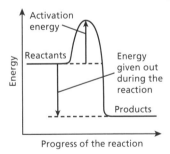

Exam practice questions

1.

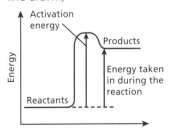

(1 mark for more than one polymer chain; 1 mark for smaller lines connecting the polymer chains; 1 mark for ordered structure) **[3]**

2.

(1 mark for line starting at origin; 1 mark for steeper curve; 1 mark for lines finishing at the same height) **[3]**

3.

(1 mark for products lower than reactants; 1 mark for activation energy shown; 1 mark for energy pathway line drawn) **[3]**

4.

(1 mark for products higher than reactants; 1 mark for activation energy shown) **[2]**

Pages 58–61: Label
Complete the example
3. **a)** *See label below.* (*Accept* Bunsen burner)
   b) *See label below.* (*Accept* condenser)

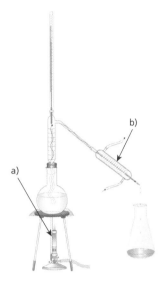

4.

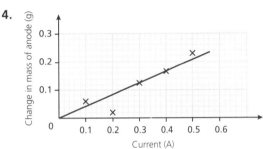

Exam practice questions
1.

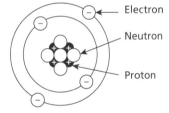

(1 mark for 'proton' correctly labelled; 1 mark for 'neutron' correctly labelled) **[2]**
2. **a)** *See label below.* **[1]**
   b) *See label below.* **[1]**

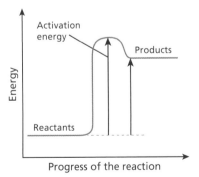

3. **a)** *See label below.* [1]
b) *See label below.* [1]

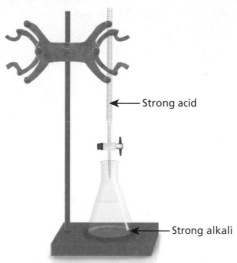

Strong acid

Strong alkali

4. *1 mark for the 78.08% section labelled as* nitrogen *or* N_2*; 1 mark for the 20.95% section labelled as* oxygen *or* O_2*; 1 mark for the 0.93% section labelled as* argon *or* Ar [3]

Pages 62–65: Suggest
Complete the example
3. Co^{2+} and Co^{3+}
4. **a)** *Any one from:* less blue; becomes colourless
b) *Any one from:* didn't stir the solution correctly; the bulb of the thermometer was not in the solution

Exam practice questions
1. **a)** Too soft [1]
b) As an alloy (with silver, copper and zinc) (*Accept* formulation / mixture with other metals) [1]
2. Measuring the mass loss as the reaction happens. [1]
Measuring the volume of gas produced during the reaction. [1]
3. **a)** Covalent [1]
b) Giant (covalent) / giant covalent structure / macromolecule [1]
4. **a)** Pipette [1]
b) *Any two from:* Swirl on the addition of the acid; white tile under the conical flask; add drop near the end point; use wash bottle to add washings into conical flask between additions of acid. [2]
c) mol/dm³ [1]
g/dm³ [1]
5. **a)** Contains only hydrogen and carbon. [1]
Contains C=C bonds [1]
b) Poly(styrene) melts / Thermosoftening polymers melt but thermosetting polymers do not. [1]
Therefore poly(styrene) / thermosoftening polymers can be re-shaped into new products but thermosetting polymers cannot. [1]

Pages 66–71: Explain
Complete the example
2. **Filter** the mixture.
Collect the **solid** in the filter paper.
As calcium carbonate is **insoluble**, this is the solid.
3. In a chemical reaction, no **atoms** are lost or made. The atoms are just rearranged and so the mass of the products **equals** the mass of the reactants. But in the decomposition of copper(II) carbonate it looks like the mass **decreases**. This is because a **gas** is made which will go into the air. So, the mass of the solid product is **less** than the mass of the solid reactant and you do not measure the mass of the gas lost to the **air**.

Exam practice questions
1. Oxygen is added to the metal. [1]
2. **a)** Metal atoms lose (outer shell) electrons [1]
to become positive ions. [1]
b) Non-metal atoms gain (outer shell) electrons [1]
to become negative ions. [1]
3. **a)** *Four from:* The atoms get larger / atomic radii increase; [4]
Less attraction between the (positive) nucleus and (outer shell) electrons;
Outer shell electrons are more easily lost;
To become a positive / 1+ ion; More reactive as you go down the group.
b) The atoms get larger / Atomic radii increase. [1]
Less attraction from the (positive) nucleus to attract / gain an electron [1]
Less reactive as you go down the group [1]
to become a negative/1– ion. [1]
c) Atoms have a stable arrangement of electrons. (*Accept* full outer shell (of electrons)) [1]
4. **a)** Particles have more kinetic energy. [1]
More collisions in the same time. [1]
More collisions have higher energy / More collisions occur or exceed the activation energy. [1]
More successful collisions in the same time. [1]
b) Powder has more surface area than ribbon. [1]
More particles exposed for collision at the same time. [1]
More successful collisions in the same amount of time. [1]
5. **a)** Ions free to move. [1]
To carry charge / allow current to flow. [1]
b) Cryolite lowers the melting point. [1]
Reduces energy use / operating temperature / cost. [1]
c) Oxygen is formed (at the anode). [1]
Reacts (immediately) with the carbon of the anode. [1]
Makes carbon dioxide that is released into the atmosphere. [1]
Carbon anode burns away / gets smaller. [1]
6. ***Level 3 (5–6 marks):*** *Relevant points (reasons / causes) are identified, given in detail and logically linked to form a clear account.*

Level 2 (3–4 marks): Relevant points (reasons / causes) are identified, and there are attempts at logical linking. The resulting account is not fully clear.

Level 1 (1–2 marks): Points are identified and stated simply, but their relevance is not clear and there is no attempt at logical linking.

Indicative content:

In diamond:

Many strong covalent bonds

need to be broken / overcome

this takes a lot of energy

In methane:

Weak forces of attraction / intermolecular forces

between the molecules

need to be overcome / no covalent bonds are broken and

this requires a lower amount of energy

Conclusion: So, the melting point of methane is lower than diamond.

7. Amount (mol) = mass(g)/M_r or A_r **[1]**
   There is 1 mole of copper(II) sulfate. **[1]**
   There is 0.5 mole of Fe. **[1]**
   From the equation the mole ratio is 1 : 1 **[1]**
   Fe is used up / $CuSO_4$ is left behind. **[1]**
   Therefore the limiting reactant is Fe. **[1]**

8. a) Fully ionises **[1]**
   in solution / water. **[1]**
   b) Solution A has a concentration of
   36.5 ÷ 1000 = 0.0365 g/cm³ **[1]**
   Solution B has a concentration of
   18.25 ÷ 250 = 0.073 g/cm³ **[1]**
   Solution B is more concentrated than solution A. /
   Solution A is more dilute than solution B. **[1]**

Pages 72–75: Show

Complete the example

3. Percentage yield =
   $$\frac{\text{mass of actual product made}}{\text{maximum theoretical yield of product}} \times 100$$
   $$= (\frac{\mathbf{15.8}}{\mathbf{63.5}}) \times 100$$
   $$= \mathbf{24.881\ 189}, \text{ which rounds to 25\%}$$

4. 1 mol/dm³ has 1 mole of NaOH per **1** dm³ of solution.
   40 g/dm³ has **40** g of NaOH per 1 dm³ of solution.
   M_r of NaOH = **23 + 16 + 1 = 40**
   1 mole of NaOH has a mass of **40** g

Exam practice questions

1. 20% oxygen **[1]**
   80 : 20 **[1]**
   = 8 : 2 = 4 : 1 **[1]**
2. ammonium chloride ⇌ ammonia + hydrogen chloride **[1]**
3. 125 – 81 = mass of carbon dioxide **[1]**
   = 44 g **[1]**
4. M_r of Fe_2O_3 = 160 **[1]**
   Moles Fe_2O_3 = 1500 ÷ 160 = 9.375 mol **[1]**
   Mole ratio is 2 : 1 so need at least 9.375 × 2 = 18.75 mol **[1]**
   Mass of Al needed = 18.75 × 27 = 506.25 g **[1]**
   which is more than 0.5 kg, so Al is the limiting reagent. **[1]**

5. White precipitate with sodium hydroxide solution means that it could be calcium, magnesium or aluminium ions. **[1]**
   Precipitate did not re-dissolve on excess sodium hydroxide solution being added, so must be magnesium ion. **[1]**
   No colour in flame test means it could be calcium or aluminium. **[1]**
   White precipitate with silver nitrate means a chloride ion is present. **[1]**

6. *You should draw a structural formula to show the reaction:*
$$CH_2{=\!=}CH_2 + Br_2 \rightarrow CH_2{-\!-}CH_2$$
with Br, Br on lower bonds **[1]**

   Annotate the diagram with:
   Addition of bromine across the double bond **[1]**
   Only single bonds in the product **[1]**

Pages 76–79: Determine

Complete the example

3. a) Mean rate of reaction = change in mass ÷ **time**
   $$= \mathbf{0.2 \div 20 = 0.01\ g/s}$$
   b) **80** seconds

4. a) C_nH_{2n}
   b)

$$H-\overset{\overset{\displaystyle H}{|}}{\underset{\underset{\displaystyle H}{|}}{C}}-\overset{\overset{\displaystyle H}{|}}{\underset{\underset{\displaystyle H}{|}}{C}}-H$$

Exam practice questions

1. Volume of a cube = height × length × width
   $$= 30 \times 30 \times 30$$ **[1]**
   $$= 27\ 000\ nm^3 \text{ (1 mark for 27 000;}$$
   1 mark for nm³) **[2]**

2. a) Metal **[1]**
   b) °C **[1]**
   c) Calcium, cobalt, copper (*Accept* Ca, Co *and* Cu) **[1]**

3. Mass of iron used = 106.00 – 50.00 = 56 g **[1]**
   Moles of iron used = $\frac{56}{56}$ = 1 mole **[1]**
   Mass of oxygen used = 130 – 106 = 24 g **[1]**
   Moles of oxygen molecules = $\frac{24}{32}$ = 0.75 moles **[1]**
   So, there is a mole ratio of 4 : 3 of iron : oxygen molecules **[1]**
   The product has the empirical formula Fe_2O_3 and so the balanced equation is: $4Fe + 3O_2 \rightarrow 2Fe_2O_3$ **[1]**

4. moles = concentration × volume **[1]**
   $10 \times \frac{0.05}{1000}$ = 0.0005 moles of sulfuric acid **[1]**
   Ratio is 1 : 2 for sulfuric acid: potassium hydroxide **[1]**
   So will need 0.001 moles of potassium hydroxide **[1]**
   $$\frac{\text{moles}}{\text{concentration}} = \text{volume}$$
   $$= \frac{0.001}{0.12 \times 1000} \times 1000 = 8.33\ cm^3$$ **[1]**

Pages 80–81: Balance

Complete the example

3. $N_2 + 3H_2 \rightleftharpoons \mathbf{2NH_3}$
4. $4OH^- \rightarrow O_2 + \mathbf{2H_2O + 4e^-}$

Exam practice questions

1. $4Li + O_2 \rightarrow 2Li_2O$ [1]
2. $C_2H_5OH + 3O_2 \rightarrow 2CO_2 + 3H_2O$ [1]
3. a) $2Cl^- \rightarrow Cl_2 + 2e^-$ [1]
   b) $Cu^{2+} + 2e^- \rightarrow Cu$ [1]

Pages 82–85: Calculate

Complete the example

3. $12 + (2 \times 16) = 44$
4. a) M_r of $Fe_2O_3 = (2 \times 56) + (3 \times 16) = 160$

   % Fe $= \dfrac{2 \times 56}{160} \times 100 = 70\%$

   b) % yield = Mass of product actually made ÷ Maximum theoretical mass of product × 100

   Moles of iron(III) oxide used $= \dfrac{320 \times 1000 \times 1000}{160}$
   $= 2\,000\,000$ moles

   Mole ratio iron(III) oxide : iron is 1 : 2

   So maximum number of moles of iron that can be made $= 4\,000\,000$ moles

   Theoretical yield $= 4\,000\,000 \times 56 = 224\,000\,000$ g
   $= 224$ tonnes

   % yield $= \dfrac{224}{320} \times 100 = 70\%$

Exam practice questions

1. Height × base × width / 2 × 2 × 2 [1]
   $= 8$ nm³ [1]
2. Quantity of product formed $= 404.80 - 403.65 = 1.15$ g [1]

   Mean rate of reaction $= \dfrac{\text{quantity of product formed}}{\text{time}}$ or

   Mean rate of reaction $= \dfrac{1.15}{90} = 0.012\,777\,78$ [1]
   $= 0.0128$ g/s [2]

   (1 mark for 0.0128; 1 mark for g/s)
3. a) $14 + (3 \times 1) = 17$ [1]
   b) (mass of nitrogen ÷ relative formula mass of ammonia) × 100 or $\dfrac{14}{17} \times 100$ [1]
   $= 82\%$ (Accept 82.4%) [1]
4. a) $M_r = 25.5 + 1 = 36.5$ [1]
   Number of moles $= \dfrac{\text{mass}}{M_r}$ [1]

   $= \dfrac{1.825}{36.5} = 0.05$ mol [1]

   b) 1 dm³ = 1000 cm³ [1]
   1.825×2 [1]
   $= 3.65$ g/dm³ [1]

   c) Number of moles = concentration × volume

   Concentration = volume ÷ number of moles [1]
   $= 0.05 \div 0.5$
   $= 0.1$ mol/dm³ [1]

Pages 86–89: Plan

Complete the example

3. Add the same mass and **surface area** of metals to the same **volume** and concentration of (dilute) nitric acid.
   Observe the temperature change or the number of **bubbles**.
   Determine conclusion:
   - Silver has no reaction.

   - Zinc has some bubbles and **an increase** in temperature.
   - Calcium has **lots of bubbles** and the **greatest increase** in temperature.

4. Put a measured volume of sodium thiosulfate into a **(conical) flask**.
   Add a measured volume of hydrochloric acid.
   Immediately put the reaction vessel on a **cross** or between **light sensors** and start a **stopwatch**.
   Measure the time for the **cross** to become no longer **visible**.
   Repeat and find the **mean**.
   Repeat for different **concentrations** of sodium thiosulfate.

Exam practice questions

1. **Level 2 (3–4 marks):** Valid logical method.
   Level 1 (1–2 marks): Method has some relevant steps but not a valid outcome and may not be logical or clear.
   Indicative content:
   Use a clean, dry nichrome wire loop.
   Put the wire loop into the solution.
   Put the solution into the blue Bunsen flame.
   Observe the colour.
   If the colour is green, copper ions are present.

2. **Level 3 (5–6 marks):** The method would lead to the production of a valid outcome. All key steps are identified and logically sequenced.
   Level 2 (3–4 marks): The method would not necessarily lead to a valid outcome. Most steps are identified, but the method is not fully logically sequenced.
   Level 1 (1–2 marks): The method would not lead to a valid outcome. Some relevant steps are identified, but links are not made clear.
   Indicative content:
   Add excess copper(II) oxide to sulfuric acid.
   Stir.
   Filter off the excess copper(II) oxide.
   Collect the filtrate.
   Heat to half the volume.
   Allow to crystalise.
   Remove crystals and pat dry with absorbent paper / Put in a drying oven.

3. **Level 3 (5–6 marks):** The method would lead to the production of a valid outcome. All key steps are identified and logically sequenced.
   Level 2 (3–4 marks): The method would not necessarily lead to a valid outcome. Most steps are identified, but the method is not fully logically sequenced.
   Level 1 (1–2 marks): The method would not lead to a valid outcome. Some relevant steps are identified, but links are not made clear.
   Indicative content:
   Collect up to four samples of each gas.
   As soon as the gas has been identified, no further tests are needed.

The tests are:

Put a lighted splint in the test tube and if you hear a pop hydrogen has been identified.

Put a glowing splint in the test tube and if it relights oxygen has been identified.

Put in damp litmus paper and replace the stopper. If it bleaches, chlorine has been identified.

Add a pipette of limewater and replace the stopper. Shake and if it goes cloudy then the gas is carbon dioxide.

4. **Level 3 (5–6 marks):** *The method would lead to the production of a valid outcome. All key steps are identified and logically sequenced.*

   Level 2 (3–4 marks): *The method would not necessarily lead to a valid outcome. Most steps are identified, but the method is not fully logically sequenced.*

   Level 1 (1–2 marks): *The method would not lead to a valid outcome. Some relevant steps are identified, but links are not made clear.*

   Indicative content:

   Filter the sea water to remove sand.

   Measure the volume of the sample of water.

   Ensure mass measurement is in g.

   Ensure volume measurement is in dm^3.

   Gently heat.

   Evaporate all of the water away / Ensure residue is dry by using a drying oven / Pat dry with absorbent paper.

   Measure the mass of the dry residue / solid.

   Calculate the concentration of the salt by:

   Concentration (g/dm³) = mass of residue (g) ÷ volume (dm³)

Pages 90–95: Plot

Complete the example

2.

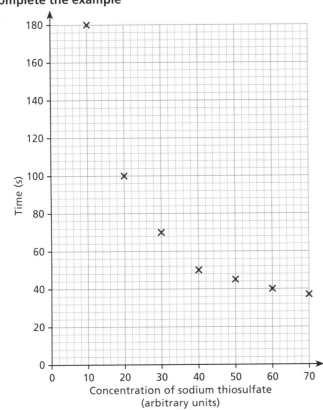

3.

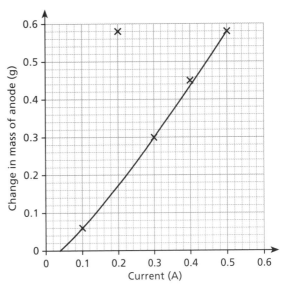

Exam practice questions

1. *Data plotted correctly with correct label as shown.* **[1]**

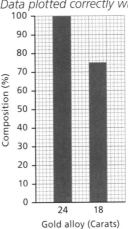

2. *All points plotted correctly as shown (±½ small squares).*
   (Allow 1 mark if five or six points are correctly plotted.) **[2]**

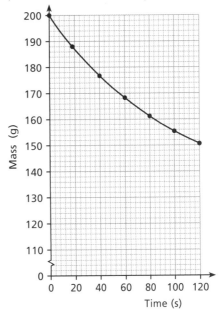

3. *Sensible scales, using at least half the grid for the points.* **[1]**
   All points plotted correctly as shown (±½ small squares). **[2]**
   (Allow 1 mark if five or six of the points are correct.)

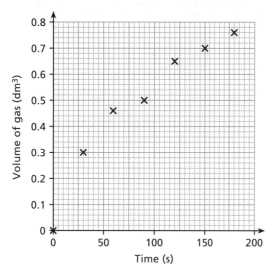

Pages 96–99: Compare

Complete the example

2. Covalent bonds are stronger than intermolecular forces.
3. Both ethene and ethane are **hydrocarbons**, which are made of only carbon and hydrogen held together by **covalent** bonds. Both ethene and ethane are small **molecules**. Although both ethene and ethane have **two** carbon atoms in each molecule, **ethene** contains a C=C double bond, whereas **ethane** only has single bonds.

Exam practice questions

1. The surface area to volume ratio of a coarse particle is 10 times smaller than that of a fine particle. **[1]**
2. *Level 2 (3–4 marks): Valid comparison between the two molecules with both similarities and differences stated.*
   Level 1 (1–2 marks): Some correct statements about each molecule. Comparison is not fully clear.
   Indicative content:
   All contain only carbon atoms.
   All contain covalent bonds.
   All saturated (only contain single bonds).
   Diamond and graphite are giant covalent structures.
   Buckminsterfullerene is a simple molecule.
   Graphite and buckminsterfullerene have three covalent bonds on every carbon atom, whereas diamond has four covalent bonds on every carbon atom.
   Graphite has layers (planes) of atoms that can easily slide, whereas diamond and buckminsterfullerene do not.
   Graphite has electrons that are free to move, whereas diamond and buckminsterfullerene do not.
   Buckminsterfullerene makes a 3D cage, whereas graphite and diamond do not.
3. *Level 3 (5–6 marks): A detailed and logical comparison is given, which demonstrates a broad knowledge and understanding of the key scientific ideas.*
   Level 2 (3–4 marks): A description which shows reasonable knowledge and understanding of the key scientific ideas. Comparisons are made but may not contain all the information to make a clear comparison.
   Level 1 (1–2 marks): Simple statements are made which demonstrate a basic knowledge of some of the relevant ideas.

Indicative content:
Both transition metals and Group 1 metals make positive ions.
Transition metals have high melting points, whereas Group 1 metals have low melting points.
Transition metals have high densities whereas Group 1 metals have low densities.
Transition metals are strong and hard whereas Group 1 metals are soft.
Transition metals have low reactivity / react slowly (with water or oxygen) whereas Group 1 metals react quickly with water or oxygen.
Transition metals are used as catalysts whereas Group 1 metals are not.
Transition metals make more than one stable ion whereas Group 1 metals make only 1+ ions.
Transition metals make coloured compounds whereas Group 1 metals make white compounds.

4. *Level 2 (3–4 marks): Valid comparison between the two types of polymer, with both similarities and differences stated.*
   Level 1 (1–2 marks): Some correct statements about each type of polymer. Comparison is not fully clear.
   Indicative content:
   Both polymer chains are made from small repeating units.
   Both polymers are very large molecules.
   For both polymers, the atoms in the polymer chains are held together by covalent bonds.
   There are weaker, intermolecular forces between the polymer chains in the thermosoftening polymer, but there are strong covalent bonds between the polymer chains in the thermosetting polymers.

Pages 100–103: Estimate

Complete the example

2. Between 63 and 64

Exam practice questions

1. *Accept any number between –41 and 25°C.* **[1]**
2. *Accept any number less than 1.* **[1]**
3. *Accept a number between –119 and 24°C.* **[1]**
4. a) *Accept a number between 85% and 90%* **[1]**
   b) *Accept an answer between $\frac{1}{9}$ and $\frac{1}{13}$* **[1]**
5. $0.05 \div 4.2 \times 100$ **[1]**
   $= 1\%$ **[1]**

Pages 104–107: Predict

Complete the example

2. Grey / Black solid
3. **Less** sulfur dioxide will be made. The **endothermic / backwards** reaction will be favoured.

Exam practice questions

1. a) Changes colour / Becomes covered in a rose coloured solid **[1]**
   b) From blue **[1]**
      to colourless **[1]**
2. a) It will increase the rate of reaction. **[1]**
   b) The same maximum mass will be produced. **[1]**
   c) It will increase the rate of reaction. **[1]**